T0149718

What an absolute honour to be asked to write a note about my dear friend Rods amazing work. Truly an angel on earth who speaks words of pure light that must be of Divine origins. His words are inspirational and motivating.

They make the journey we call life just a little bit clearer. Rod has definitely been an inspiration to my own personal healing and growth. When someone uses their gifts and shares them with others the vibration of those around them is raised and the entire planet receives the benefits. I am filled with an overflow of gratitude to bear witness to such a gift as it expands. Thank you Rod xx.

Julie Gorton,
Reiki Master,
Intuitive Energy Healer,
Crystal Therapist,
Spiritual Counsellor,
Meditation and Mindfulness Coach.
http://www.juliegorton.com

If you have been drawn to buy "Where you open is where you are at" either for yourself or for a friend it is likely due to the fact that you have connected into Rod's energy. This book combines direct material from the Universe, God, your higher power, and insights that Rod has become aware of throughout his journey. I have known Rod for over 10 years and have watched as he has peeled back the layers of judgement, of limited perception, of hurt, of joy, of wonder. We all have these layers, however, it takes true unconditional love and courage for the self and for others to unpeel them and then to openly share that journey.....warts and all.

Rod has shared his journey and with each step connected to someone who is also facing similar trials and tribulations. He connects through words and song the message that we are all great, unique and a treasure. We, at times, act in ways we later may wish we didn't, however Rod reminds us that without these challenges we do not grow. May this book and further work of Rodney's help you in your own journey? May you find a word or phrase or titbit that helps you through?

Debra Mc Cormick
BMS and MBA Macquarie University
Vedic Master Chopra University
Founder Soul Inspiration and Teach Kids Yoga
International Author and Speaker on Children's Holistic Wellbeing, Yoga and Higher Consciousness

Rod would like to acknowledge and thank from the deepest part of his heart the beautiful words shared and unconditional love both Julie and Debra possess, and our mutual love and friendship. Julie and Debra are of pure beauty and share with the world the gifts they also possess, to assist in the world and its inhabitants shining and generating and understanding the truth of love and happiness. xx

A huge thankyou to Julie Gorton for her kindness and generosity in going over all the elements of the book, proofing and editing and ironing out any bugs, for which I am deeply grateful. xx

Rod would also like to share the concept of the book was inspired by a conversation he was having with his beautiful friend Cindy Wenban, and how the quotes could be presented to the world in a book form? And 'Where You Open Is Where You're At' was born. Thanks Cindy for your love and friendship xx

The photos in the book were taken by Rod's great friend Jenni Mac. Jenni & Rod studied two degrees together, and have become the greatest of friends, where only love and beautiful connection exists. Jenni certainly sees the world through a special lens, and Rod is so honoured that Jenni agreed to allow the quotes to be written on her photos and shared throughout the book. Only love and admiration. Thankyou Jenni from the deepest part of my heart. Love you xx

WHERE YOU OPEN IS WHERE YOU'RE AT

A Universal Guide To Healing

ROD PAINTER

BALBOA.
PRESS
A DIVISION OF HAY HOUSE

Balboa Press books may be ordered through booksellers or by contacting:

Balboa Press
A Division of Hay House
1663 Liberty Drive
Bloomington, IN 47403
www.balboapress.com.au
1 (877) 407-4847

Print information available on the last page.

ISBN: 978-1-5043-1195-3 (sc)
ISBN: 978-1-5043-1194-6 (e)

Balboa Press rev. date: 01/31/2018

I dedicate this book to the most amazing, beautiful, and influential person in my world: my mum, Stephanie Dolores Painter (1/8/1929–25/8/2003). I will love you forever.

XX

Introduction

I can remember from an early time in my life—I think as a teenager—words would just miraculously appear, and without filter, I would say them. I had no idea where the complex sentences came from, but unobstructed, they poured out. At first, I enjoyed speaking these words and shared them with anyone who would listen. I had no idea that these words were for a greater purpose—gifts, so to speak.

My own voice even woke me up as I slept. Initially, I believed in my intellect, but I soon realised that I was masquerading as something I was not, and I felt like a fraud. My internal dialogue started to say things like "Who do you think you are?" and "You have no right or intelligence to converse with people, especially qualified people, in such a way!"

I had a feeling deep within I regularly ignored—the feeling that I was supposed to help others. But I believed I was not worthy due to my limited education, and I did not think I possessed the intelligence to even venture down the road to becoming qualified. I believed that because I grew up in a government-housing suburb, I wasn't worthy. I wasn't permitted to associate with educated people, let alone share my words. So I set my sights on a life of mediocrity. As a result, words stopped flowing, and it parked any ambition.

Although I say that, my life became good. I had a great job working for the government, and I grew more confident in my own skin. I started a beautiful family, bringing into the world two amazing sons, who really changed the way I viewed myself. I had a deep desire to make them proud and lead by example, but self-belief that didn't exist compressed the prospect. I still had something missing. I remember telling my mum many times, "One day, I'll make you proud and go to university," but of course, with life so busy and my lack of self-belief, I pursued no action—not until heartbreak occurred. In 2003, my mum passed away, and it rocked my world to its foundation.

present itself. It may be subtle, but when you're prepared, you will pick up on these visions or opportunities, a bit like intuition or a sixth sense. Stay open to these opportunities, and allow them to flow through you. Before you fall into the peace and tranquillity of meditation, request to know your purpose, and just give in to the response. The answer is awaiting your question.

Knowledge of the Universe flows within us. It's not separate from us, as if we have to travel somewhere to find it. We can tap into this abundance of knowledge and happiness, peace, and prosperity; we just have to ask. When things get tough, ask for an answer. Lie back and float for a while, and don't allow the overlapping confusion to chew you up. Give in to the Collectiveness, and the answers will be there.

Throughout the book, I have weaved in the terms *Universe, Collectiveness, core, divinity, intuition, guidance, spirit, enlightenment, source, magic, gift,* and *God* and many more terms. And we may even have to use other terms. But the one constant here is that we have a greater purpose and connectiveness, and we all may know it by many names; however, it always means the exact same thing, and that's the place where love is born.

This is your journey. Choose to read *Where You Open Is Where You're At: A Universal Guide to Healing* from front to back, or open it up wherever you feel guided to start. Close your eyes, turn to a page, and start your day with love, gratitude, and an open heart. Be kind, generous, and thankful, and you'll see what an amazing and beautiful existence we all share.

With love, thanks, gratitude, and heart,

Your friend Rod XXOO

Some days, we wake feeling as if we have the whole world sitting on our shoulders, not really knowing why but perhaps in the process reflecting on our self-worth and purpose. Maybe a moment of turmoil recently presented itself to us, and even though it is not easily recognisable, if we reflect for a moment, the catalyst of the turmoil appears. Is the catalyst something we've done? An expectation we placed on ourselves? An expectation from another?

At this exact moment, we have the opportunity to stay present in the here and now. We can remain mindful that this issue is exactly what it is—not the now, not the here. It's OK to be perfectly present, but it doesn't help to beat ourselves up about truly unimportant things. The presence of the feelings of now, and being mindful brings us back to the centre, jolts us into realisation, and gives us an opportunity. Meditation is a key, so to speak, to open the door to our inner understanding; here, our clarity, peace, and ultimate happiness will reveal themselves.

Truth lies at the core, the section that once connected

to the source. The flesh is the transformation from

one realm to the next; however, humanity, when in

this form, can flitter in the flesh and lose sight of that

connectedness that we once had. If one solely exists in

the flesh without an inner awareness of the beauty that

provides the pure nutrition of our existence, then one

can wilt away and decay, and other entities that feed off

our malaise can fill up the decayed flesh.

We can, however, feed off our experiences of the flesh,

gaining nutrition that moves us and generates wisdom

and knowing of the self, and the more of that nutrition

we eat, the closer we get. At the core, seeds of love are

born, and sharing these seeds plants them in the soil

for future growth and the plantation of love to be born.

We are that apple of his eye, sharing love with the world.

Within our minds, we have a superhighway of
thoughts, actions, struggles, habits (good and bad),
emotions, and feelings. The depth of unknowing of
the superhighway goes on, but its infrastructure is
highly intuitive. Construction of these roads happens
constantly. The single-lane road that gets the most
usage will have the most funding and hence turn into
the two-lane road, the three-lane road, and in some
cases the superhighway. Now, this complexity may be
a great thing for highly functioning individuals, but
when the infrastructure's reinforcement and increase in
carriageway result from maladaptive, negative, flawed,
and addictive behaviour, stoplights stay green, and no
other traffic can merge. And when the peak hour sparks
up, it pushes everything else into a parking lot or dead-
end street.

We know when we are consumed by unhealthy actions,
but we often feel we have no control to stop them.
We need to learn how to slow down that catapulting
traffic, fix the traffic lights, and give those backstreets
some usage, as we form new, positive habits there if we
invest in those roads. Explore the inner self through
meditation, and open all roads for exploration and
ultimate exposure to greatness. Think of the mind as
a road map, and focus more attention on love, health,
interests, relationships, family, friends, and passions.
Give time to the pursuit of your happiness; this will
then generate that greater portion toward this success.

Also, try to keep your vehicle contained and to not
drive aimlessly and recklessly into traffic, as this takes
away your power and control. When you are invited into
another's city streets, drive carefully and respectfully,
and if your vehicle appears to start to drive in negative
autopilot, turn it off, and shut it down until control
returns. Enjoy this beautiful ride of self-discovery. I
wish you nothing but love, happiness, and good health.

As our suit of humanity becomes fatigued and loses its capacity to maintain itself in the expanse of the Universe, like a newly born hatchling, the soul strips back the remaining shell and re-enters from where it once came. Our human shell is as tough as it is fragile, and the manifested human intellect is designed to keep the vehicle functioning with as minimal input as possible, whilst we navigate and explore our purpose before our ultimate return.

My clarity was reinforced today whilst I was with one particular woman I love, admire, and cherish with all my heart. The connection between us two is only one, and all our human purpose is love. When one has love, kindness, understanding, and a heart that openly appreciates the ebbs and flows, only peace prevails. And the resultant waves of beauty and healing, even without one knowing it, assist the world in becoming a more inhabitable and loving landscape whilst we explore that meaning.

We have no divide—no us and them—but function as a collective of entities attempting to navigate their way before their return. If you are love, give love, embrace love, and teach love, only love will be, and when that time comes for our return, we can all open our arms and hearts, transition peacefully, and celebrate the beauty just had, connecting all with love.

As each golden rose petal peels back, exposing the next, the soul gets closer to its maker. This sends a waft of a beautiful fragrance, like a smoke signal, to family already there, alerting of your return home. Whilst that bud blossoms into our beautiful perfection, we must nurture our soil, creating that fragrance, whilst we remain here to spread love, wisdom, kindness, and generosity to all corners, as if in a protective cocoon.

This constant connection contributes to our ultimate happiness, and if we neglect it, we lose the connection, and human problems manifest. Fear of our greater connection and ultimate human limitations contribute to our disconnection, which moves us away from where pure love truly resonates from.

When one lives in a space of purity—as you did, Aunty Aud—fear has no place, and only love exists. You have taught me so much about love, purity, kindness, and generosity. And every single person who had the honour to meet you felt your love and gentleness. There will only ever be one Aunty Aud. You were not just our aunty; you were our surrogate mum, grandma, and confidante, and we are all so blessed to call you ours, but we know you have greater things to do separate from this world. You were an angel on Earth whose last petal has fallen, returning to the source. We'll all miss and love you forever—feeling so, so sad but so much love.

When we smell your fragrance, we'll know you're near, watching over us, protecting us, and connecting with us.

Passion is a beautiful human condition that can contribute to one's greatness and ultimate human success. Passion in romance can also feel electrifying, however counterintuitive in its essence. But passion sits on the high end of a spectrum and generally creates this euphoria due to the associated lows that can accompany passion at its alternative and extreme end.

Humans mistake passion and its polar divides for love; however, love is gentle, calm, peaceful, consistent, and safe. The extremes on both ends dissipate, and only beauty prevails when pure love is present. Wisdom certainly allows us to see that we need the presence of a balanced equilibrium with all things, bringing the extremes closer to the middle and taking off the confusing edge.

Some still crave the addictive aspects of romantic passion, but when things no longer constantly reach a positive peak, the complete opposite accompanies passion; a deep despair prevails. I certainly know which option I'd choose. How about you? Would you choose love, peace, happiness, calmness, safety, gentleness, connectedness, commitment, and the sharing of beauty?

No matter what's happening in one's world, the default

point of kindness will serve one well. Kindness is that

building block that transforms one's mountain of

despair into a beacon that radiates love and healing

into the world for the beacon again to return home to

its creator. If we visualise our mountain of despair as

a radio tower sending out waves of kindness and love,

we'll see how the tower's waves bounce off all that they

come in contact with, ricochet in all directions, and

touch all in their path, both physical and spiritual. It's

clear the kindness and love will return home.

These blankets of love have dominance over despair and

its accompanying turmoil, sending beauty throughout

the world and nullifying the ugliness that can exist

if we fail to combat it with love. Sending waves of

energetic love from my mountain tower to all provides

healing, peace, and kindness and contributes to a

beautiful and magical love- and kindness-filled day.

We are all made of many characteristics, interests, loves, passions, and gifts. At times, we wonder what the differences are all about, and we reflect on our inadequacies, especially in comparison to others' gifts. But we never have to compare our many characteristic elements or measure them against another's qualities to validate our place in the world. If we strip back all that we do, the default point should take us back to exactly where we all derived from.

That place of love and kindness exists in us all; however, the ravages of our humanity can tarnish it, and their residual weight can sit heavily on our psyche. When we find ourselves in a tarnished place, we should reflect on our core and embrace our individual qualities. Meditation supports alignment and peace and can assist in bringing our angst to a place of calm, self-validation, and love. Wind down your bucket into your well of love, and wind it back up to embrace and incorporate love into all facets of your being.

Feeling my whole body beat to the rhythm of my heart, I slow my heartbeat down to meet the timing of my breath. I immerse myself deeply in this space and find comfort as I acknowledge its purpose and meaning. And as my beating heart, my body, and my mind align with my similarly paced breath, I sense I become a beacon of energy, sending waves of sonar energy and pulses of love out into the Universe so entities requiring healing and nurturing can absorb them.

As these energetic pulses bounce, they are magnified and split, sending multiple waves to all corners. Many of us feel hardened by the ravages of our humanity and find it difficult to accept our worthiness, but if we get enough love, it will soften us so we accept love. Love will then continue to perpetuate, and our rock façade will transform into a sponge that can accept all that good, pure love. Be love, accept love, and gift love so that only love fills the airways like a sonar pulse, bouncing and magnifying itself until love heals all.

Listen to your body, listen to your mind, and listen to your spirit. We constantly talk to ourselves to find alignment, perfection for healing, and our ultimate happiness, but we still get caught up in grandiose expectations and feel like a failure when we miss these great heights. Our malaise at times results from not hearing our internal talk and not taking action when required. We need not to conquer the world, but to conquer our hearts, minds, and spirits. We need to discover what's within us, not what's around us.

At times, the urge to look within us guides us to human greatness, and that's wonderful. We are all on that spectrum and divine in essence. And for others, it is as simple as going within for their own internal greatness, finding that place that generates their peace; from this platform, they resurrect their self-love and love for all. Our purposes vary; nonetheless, each carries importance. What we may perceive as simplistic may, in fact, represent the greatest gift we all have to give.

While our light illuminates the path we must travel, an unsuspecting soul may need to step into the light of love generated by another to have his or her blinkers removed. Gently does it, and be kind to yourself. Do as you do at your pace. Go within, find the deep beauty that exists within us all, and shine your light of love onto the world.

An expanse exists outside our bubble, and ideally, our protective bubble should exist throughout our human passage, slowly decaying to align us with our return back to the collective spirit. However, many of our bubbles get disrupted or burst before their natural existence has run its course, leaving our spirits floating aimlessly without guidance or direction.

Generally, these disturbances occur due to some form of trauma. As a result of the trauma, our spirit gets released early and lacks preparedness because it is shocked, confused, and isolated, similar to a bird falling from its nest before it's ready to fly. The bird either successfully flies and lands or fails to and gets injured, gets attacked by predators, and doesn't have the necessary skills to blossom into what it was destined to become whilst here on Earth.

The difference for us, as humans, is that we have been gifted an intellect, and if trauma cracks our egg before it's ready to hatch, the trauma will, in actual fact, provide us with access to that exact expanse before lineal time presents itself. The world and the Universe are our oysters. When presented with a traumatic scenario, don't own trauma in isolation, as we have many gifted teachers and healers and a lot of wisdom to access that show us we can embrace trauma as a true gift. We can use it to improve our greatness and navigate the human experience. Gravitate toward love, kindness, respect, forgiveness, and peace, and seek out like-minded humans to support you through any difficult or unpredictable transition.

A warmth, gentleness, and simplicity manifest when

one lives of truth and of love. If we can learn to strip

back the build-up and residuals of our past lives

without a "What's in it for me?" mentality, a pureness of

existence will prevail. If we stay in touch with our core,

our spirit will inevitably bring us closer to the beautiful

connections we can all share, without the tarnished

ravages that our humanity can sometimes bestow on us.

Visualise immersing yourself in a deep well of love, and

allow it to detoxify you and wash away life's struggles.

Then surface back in the world rejuvenated and as

perfect as when you were born.

The power of thought can be one person's greatest gift and another's greatest burden. Thought dreams up greatness, and thought catastrophizes. Thought provides the gateway to our happiness or our sadness. To regulate and control thought may seem easy for some, and it consumes others. If we step back and reflect on our thoughts, we can see the triggers, but we need to habitually control our thoughts to regulate our happiness. When we leave thought to blow in the wind, it will go to all places—and some not always positive. Hence, angst manifests itself, and a residual sadness presents itself.

Stay mindful of what and how you think, as those thoughts will start a snowball that grows and picks up momentum, attracting all in its path. So do you want that snowball to be made of wonder, love, happiness, peace, purpose, and magic? Or sadness, worry, angst, and ill health? I have a sense of what we all would prefer. Affirmations are great reminders to keep in focus. You may find it hard to acknowledge self-love and greatness at first, but this could provide the first step to preventing self-sabotage. Stop self-sabotage, and stop your thoughts from accessing the place that feeds self-sabotage: terror.

Feed your thoughts only with love, beauty, and wonder, as what you feed thoughts is what they will become. Like people say, "You are what you eat." And we are all of love and from love, beautiful, unique, and magic all in our own special ways. Sure, we all go at different paces, and never should we compare our paces, as this again raises some toxic food for thought. Pick up on your negative thoughts, and reel them in. If you have negativities on the line, throw them back in. Only catch your greatness and beauty, and accept that as your meal for thought: nothing but love.

Having presence of being means staying mindful, respectful, and courteous and adapting to the environment we find ourselves in. It is like being an assertive driver in congested traffic and watching and manoeuvring through all others' actions to generate your own path to safety. You are the driver of your vehicle; if you let it run with you not in control, what do you think may happen?

Stay present and connected, and travel at that safe speed that generates safety. Be slow and gentle in traffic and like the wind in open spaces. Adaptability is our gift and one we must all embrace, as life will present some curveballs. If we stay rigid, we'll snap, but if we have pliability, we can sustain ourselves, sway, and adjust as the tide comes in and goes out again. This is our surety and our gift. And for certain, change will come. Our capacity to adapt will assist us in finding our balance a lot more quickly, maintaining our peace and ultimate happiness in the process.

The only thing we have complete
control of is our own choices.
As human beings we are easily
distracted by outside elements,
resulting often in emotional
turmoil. Instinctively,
heartache and sadness may be a
normal emotional reaction to
this, but when we immerse in
the energy of the emotion for a
short time and move through it,
peace, love and happiness
ultimately prevails. Rod xx

Photo - Jenni Mac

We have a thread that binds us all. Around this thread

are the experiences of our humanity—the things

that shape our egos and our identities. We measure

ourselves against others to determine our value;

however, such elements are superficial aspects of our

existence. The components made in humanity must stay

in humanity.

The only constant is this connecting thread. The thread

was here before us and will continue after our human

experience has run its course. To generate the purity of

love and happiness and experience heaven on Earth, one

must tap into the pure thread of our connecting spirit.

Meditate on this for access to the source of all.

Our purpose may not always be known, and we may not

always have the path light clear for us to find our way.

But when we pursue lives filled with kindness, love, and

gratitude, then we are already living lives of divinity.

One can only align one's reactions with the experiences

that triggered them, leading to this moment in time.

Often, one realises, sometimes immediately after an

event, that they may not have reacted in the perfect way

for what occurred. Beautiful in theory, but again, we can

only draw from that which is present at the time and

then forgive ourselves after reflection occurs later.

Of course, harm to others should never be condoned,

and one should never react with violence in any

circumstance. But the greatest life lessons come from

gaining exposure to new challenges, and this again

enhances our personal knowledge, inner growth,

and wisdom. Never own what is not yours to own,

but forgive of-the-moment decisions, when constant

learnings occur.

Immerse yourself in the beauty of love. It's as simple as that. We all have a tendency to overanalyse and complicate the simplicity of the true meaning and feeling of love. We get caught up in our heads, and our humanness fails us at times, restricting the potentially amazing connection we could have. Turmoil isn't and shouldn't be at the heart of love. Only beauty, peace, happiness and the amazing connection that love brings should.

Deeply embrace the love you already have. Hold it close to your heart, and strip away the toxins that impede your happiness. Bask in the purity, delving into the core meaning of why we're here, and retouch the essence of from where we came.

Send out your connecting love, and assist in the reconnection of love for all. Close your eyes for a moment, and truly feel the power of what love can do.

Believe in fairy tales, but don't forget getting past the

ogres before you locate the prince or princess is a bit

like a gauntlet. Don't settle; know your internal castle

is a beautiful fairy tale in itself. Never settle for second

best, as you deserve beauty, love, peace, support,

respect, and happiness. We have these internally, so

another's only purpose is to magnify them, definitely

never deplete them.

Once upon a time, all there ever was was love ...

There are jewels and precious moments that present themselves to us. Sometimes, they only appear for a moment, and in some cases a lifetime. We, at times, have a tendency to want to own the moment and never let it go, and we feel disappointed when it no longer exists. These beautiful opportunities will constantly present themselves, but we have no claims on ownership. We are only visitors here for a human time, and all that is will continue to be exactly as it's meant to be. Appreciate whilst having our human experience, that we do not own and we have no right to possess what is not ours to possess.

Love the jewels, love the moments, embrace the beauty, and appreciate the present gifts. Be mindful not to get caught up in possession, as this only contributes to heartache and despair when it's no longer there. Let things flow through, and allow them to mould naturally what is meant to be. Ongoing beauty will remain present when one's heart is open for love.

Have you ever felt you have a lot going on inside but you can't tap into the goings-on, and you ultimately feel as if your head is about to explode but you can't put your finger on why? So many words and feelings want to come through, but every time you put pen to paper, nothing wants to present itself.

We can only do our best, and it is important to keep it in perspective. The ones who love you don't care for materialism. Just enjoying your connections is the most beautiful thing to embrace. Being of love and sharing this love will break the shackles of confusion and pain of the past. As physical beings, we feel the loss of our loved ones who have passed, but this also magnifies the beauty and importance of embracing love and forgiveness whilst in the here and now.

Connect with, embrace, love, forgive, and share with your loved ones, and tell them how much they mean to you. Strip back to the core of your existence—love—and all the negative layers of your humanness will have no hold on you.

Whilst in a physical form, we have physical and psychological fluctuations. At moments, we, for no reason and with no understanding, delve into a place where happiness is complicated to define. A range of influencing factors determine these cycles of humanity.

Generally when delving and sometimes without knowledge, you may find yourself in a place of malaise. In this time, you should first be kind to your heart and spirit and focus on your awareness of the cycles. Reflect on times you have pulled through similar moments; remember not to give the cycles energy to grow and create more complications for yourself.

Keep in mind the moment in time will pass, as every other moment has passed before. In a day or two, awaken with the same spark that has always existed. Witness yourself in your interactions with others, as this can trigger that energy that grows into complications.

Be kind, gentle, loving, understanding, and patient. And all will return to perfect again.

Perfection exists right where we are. It's important, however, not to lose control of our inner knowing and awareness, as this can result in venturing beyond our core, our heart, and our spirit. We may ultimately lose our spiritual connectedness and get lured in by the attractiveness of our humanness.

To stay centred, which we can assist through meditation, keeps us grounded, balanced, and of love and purity. As long as we remain of love, kindness, and respect, then perfection exists. Shine out to the world exactly who you are. Another's measure has no weight when inner love exists.

As we commence our travels of humanity, our
suitcase of life starts to fill up. We carry this suitcase
throughout, filling it with beauty and also our
struggles. Many find that place of safety where they
can lay out and unpack their suitcase and continue
to build on their memories and experiences, sharing
with the people in their world who love, support, and
nurture them, and an inner peace prevails. Others never
unpack, never find that safe place, and start to hoard
all their experiences—good, bad, and indifferent—and
poison the beauty also mixed within.

We only have so much capacity to store experiences,
and without unpacking in that safe place, it leads to the
suitcase exploding. The Universe will always attempt
to heal the poisoned area, but we close it down, trying
to keep the case locked. Whilst we attempt to keep it at
bay, we also fail to allow beauty to enter for the risk of
the pain escaping.

A blind pimple, boil, or carbuncle will generally only
heal if it gets drawn to the surface, so if trauma exists,
even if not identified, that baggage could prevent
love and happiness from entering your world. Search
for the tool that works best for you. Is it meditation?
Counselling? We think when love presents this thing,
love generates our pain. But truly the love attempts to
heal. It just has to draw out pain to heal it.

Without self-reflection, we can at times be our own worst enemies. Right in front of us, only one tiny step away, perfection and alignment exist. But we put up walls. The walls we project certainly keep us safe, but at the same time, they limit the beauty that awaits us. Encompassing fear feeds off this reluctance to take a leap, and a potential, safe life of mediocrity subsequently holds us captive. And I'm not saying this is not beautiful for some, if not many, but if we have something constantly gnawing at our soul, then that indicates that we're destined for more we need to explore.

We're never alone when we choose to venture, and it'd surprise us to access the love that becomes present when we choose to take that step. Sure, doubters and other people wish to keep us in our place, and we need to stay mindful of their motives in the equation of life.

We must have truth within ourselves, truth in love, truth in the people who care, and truth in purpose. We are greater than we give ourselves credit for and greater than victims of our birth alignment and chosen lives. We chose these tests before our arrival, and we conquer them as part of our greater happiness whilst here on Earth.

The magnetism of love is as pure as the Universe from which we came. The energetic field love generates when it gets projected in its purest form is what we may sense as enlightenment in human form. When considering romantic love, we discover not so many dissimilarities. When north and south connect, they form a nearly unbreakable bond, and together, the magnetic and energetic fields increase and draw more into the magnetic field of love.

However, from time to time, either two souths or two norths attempt to connect, but only disconnect prevails, and an energetic push emerges. When one has an inner purity and a sound heart and spirit, one can appreciate that such connections have flaws and diminish one's beauty. No doubt, when all energies align, we all form a natural connection. One must accept self-love first and foremost so the aligning energies connect at their most beautiful and perfect place.

A family is a gift touched by the beauty of love. It has a lineage of beauty, kindness, and heart as deep as all the Universe's oceans, which we are all part of. Sure, we all get tarnished by our human experience, but if we take a step within, we can manoeuvre from our humanness for a moment and truly immerse ourselves in love. We connect on Earth only for a short time. Embrace and love your family and friends, and acknowledge their beauty, for that is the human experience. Don't let the words and experiences of love pass you by before your moment on Earth has dispersed.

Whilst in the moment, send your heart's love to your beautiful family and friends, and acknowledge your special place in my world. Make amends, and reconnect. We don't have to be right to deserve love, as love is innately ours.

Don't you just love how love feels? There's no other

feeling like it. To be immersed in such an emotion

makes you feel so alive and inspired. Feeling the love

you have for your children, family, and friends, being in

their company, and basking in their mutual love allow

your spirit to expand to touch the source from where

love originates.

We can all access this love; it's there for all of us to

embrace. We find it located in our heart when we delve

deeply within. When you tap the energy of love, you find

your passion, purpose, truth, happiness, and pure peace

of existence. You don't need to search for love, as it is

already part of your perfection. You just need to give

it permission to shine and share the glow of the magic

that makes you.

When one is of kindness, of love, and of giving, it is probably one of the greatest human gifts to give. It's important, however, to stay mindful of one's self-care, self-love, and inner kindness. A significant component and attribute of a natural healer and helper is the depletion of self. He or she gives more than he or she has and ultimately falls in a heap and gets left flat, awaiting a timely recovery period, just to do it all over again. A cycle and pattern develop here, where one doesn't wish to let anyone down or one can't say no, not wanting to hurt another's feelings or request of assistance. You must remain mindful of your fuel tank.

I have a sense that when someone's tank is full, the first half appears to take a long time to deplete; however, the second half depletes extremely quickly, and before you realise it, it requires refuelling.

Never let your inner tank go below 51 per cent full, and always allow for refuelling before offering any more support; otherwise, your tank will empty very quickly, and you will end up stranded in the middle of nowhere. Seeing this from the perspective of ownership, if someone owns 51 per cent, he or she owns the majority share. However, if you give more than your 49 per cent reserved for your support of others, then you give them ownership of the tank of your power, and then they will deplete it at will.

Maintain your power; own your heart and love. Continue to give, as that's a beautiful gift to possess, but stay mindful of yourself, of your own inner love and kindness.

Contradiction is an innate trait of humanity. We appear to constantly attempt to minimise our own contradictions by presenting to the world a different mask than what truly resonates within. We are made of many experiences—some horrific, some beautiful, and everything in between. These experiences strengthen either our ego, our spirit, our inner awareness, or our confusion. But no matter how we present ourselves to the world, we should embrace our own truth and external kindness. We don't own others' opinions of us, as only we know our path. But presenting purity of our actions and love and kindness, we can only make the world a kinder, loving, happy, and beautiful place to exist in.

Stay true to you, and shine your uniqueness on the world.

The air we can't see between us is not empty. It teems with life and with energy. All our interactions and pursuits impact all other inhabitants. Even though we may perceive the air as nothing, our actions generate waves and shifts that directly impact all other living beings. It exactly imitates the energy that we generate.

Stay mindful of the energy you emit, and attempt to only put kindness and love back into your energetic waves. This creates the higher vibrational frequency where healing manifests. To exist in this space is to exist in infinity, all connected, all loved, all purposeful, all heart, and all spirit.

All living things connect to the greatness of the

Universe. As if an hourglass, allow the gifts of the

Universe to enter your human experience for peace,

happiness, good health, purpose, and love, and stay

open to seeing we all have access to the all-knowing.

When connected, we arc as pure as the Universe itself.

All other innocent living species automatically connect,

as this is part of their spiritual evolution, but only

humans get disconnected and run misguided, aimlessly

without direction or purpose.

Through meditation, one recharges, or fills up the

human tank, so to speak. Think of meditation as the

medi-station, the service station for the spirit. It is

here one connects to the greatest and purest fuel for

a continued and purposeful human experience: that

which is love!

Humanity is like an octopus, eight arms all reaching

and searching or being consumed by something

external to themselves. These arms need to retract and

again be present and join the human core, where our

spirit resides. Whilst in spirit, we connect to all things,

and here, the octopus has the ability to again outstretch

its tentacles to gain universal knowledge, peace,

happiness, and love, as in this space, there is no core as

such, only access to all that is.

The many faces of humanity are epitomised by
the many masks we wear. We do this dance as we
manoeuvre through the many phases of our ever-
changing lives. The masks are natural traits that exist
so that we may adapt chameleon-like for the purpose
of connecting and aligning with the environments we
must navigate. The enigma that is humanity and the
complex components dispersed throughout the layers
create an inability for greater insights. We cannot gain
insights, depths of self-knowing that embrace the many
facets of who we are, and a congruence of self within all
levels of our interactions.

We can get caught up and mislead ourselves into
believing that the masks are, in fact, our complete
self, and we get lost in a falsity of only a snippet of the
greatness that truly exists within all of us.

Embrace and love and get to know all the dimensions
that make you truly whole, and stay mindful not to
get caught on the surface or on a superficial self-
belief that fails to delve deeply within. Truly knowing
yourself deeply and intimately can be scary and open
many doors of unhealed trauma, and if this is the case,
seek professional support, but here, you can have true
healing and connection to the source and locate the
depths of love.

The Uni *verse* is not unlike a verse of a song, going through the process of our greater life experience as per the nature of all in existence. Our humanity, however, is the chor *us*, for it is *us* who have been gifted the most beautiful and dynamic part of that song, where we can soar and create colour and vibrancy, and create a contagious hook filled with love, happiness, hope, and magic. The br *i*dge is where you and I stand to make our mark on the world, the captured essence that is uniquely ours and stamped with the characteristics of our individuality.

So flow with the verse of the Uni *verse*—no need to fight it, as it will be exactly what it will be. And when it comes time, our chor *us* will shine, and we'll lift and locate the beauty that has been gifted to us through our humanity, and the wave of our combined love will engulf us for the purpose of creating magic, peace, and happiness throughout the world. But the *I* in the br *i*dge is where we, as individuals, receive the opportunity to really become the guiding force that assists in shifting and moving with a dynamic structure designed to capture us and make us as creative and uplifting as we can possibly be before shifting back into the chor *us* and Uni *verse*.

Play your song, sing it loudly, dance magnificently, love deeply, be happy, get healthy, and be unique.

We are all amazing, strong, and resilient. It's

remarkable, though, how we forget to love ourselves

whilst always looking out and caring for others. Even

though others can acknowledge and appreciate that, we

fail to reinforce that within ourselves, and occasionally,

we beat ourselves up for not being worthy. We should

acknowledge others' thoughts as gifts—beautiful gifts—

but not as the definition and determining factor of our

worth. We need to gift ourselves with self-love so we can

always choose to own our heart and fill our cup on our

own terms, not terms decided by another.

What is happiness? Is it peace? Is it quiet? Is it health? Is it acquisitions? Is it money or wealth? Or is it the beauty that exists between humans, where connections occur deeply within one another, and a truth of being ignites both physically and spiritually.

Through the process of pursuing their passions, many can acquire all the fruits of humanity, and all deserve that in itself. But the true essence of happiness comes through our relationships, our families, our friends, our loved ones, and even strangers who pursue understanding the depth of our true purpose. Relationships aren't just limited to other humans. They are open to all living things, animals, nature, and our connection to the source.

First, be kind and loving to yourself. Forgive and embrace your heart, and learn and grow from the experiences that have been gifted to you. Forgive and love deeply the teachers you have had present throughout your travels, and hold, love, and nurture the beautiful family and friends who have chosen to be part of your life. This truly defines the meaning of happiness.

Pick up the phone, and call a family member or old friend you haven't contacted in a while. Don't stay too busy. Reconnect, and tell them how much you appreciate them and acknowledge the beauty they have brought to your life. To give in such a way fills the Universe with love. You have no need to expect anything in return, as the Universe already has that covered. You'll see an instantaneous return when you connect in such a way.

I would like to acknowledge my absolutely amazing and beautiful family and say thank you to them for sharing their lives with me. I embrace and give thanks for the beautiful friendships and loves that I've experienced over my lifetime, as they have all provided me with amazing learnings and challenges that have contributed to the man I am today. I feel honoured to have and grateful for my life and all that has been gifted to me.

Thank you from the deepest part of my heart.

With my love and deepest affection,

Rod XXOO

Our spirit sometimes misaligns with the body it inhabits. For many of us, our body adapts and changes as we grow, no longer a glimmer of the infant body we were once born into. Our spirit has a similar evolution and eventually returns to the source from whence it came. This beautiful and symbiotic relationship, in a lot of cases, is a natural progression and one we come to embrace and acknowledge as the passage of our humanity. But for some, the spirit's attempts to fit into that vehicle called *humanness* do not always come that easy and are fraught with inner struggles and complications that could potentially ruin that absolutely amazing and beautiful existence we are gifted to experience.

What can we do to assist us through the transitions and through the ever-changing metamorphosis that we call *humanity*? What do we have control of? We have control of our thoughts and our imagination, and therefore, we can change our views on how we can modify our human vehicle to generate a greater comfort and purpose to move through this experience with beauty and wonderment.

Close your eyes, and reconfigure. There may be some work to be had, but only you, truly deep within, know what you need to do to find that beauty, love, heart, and spirit that we all possess—until our body can no longer transition to its next phase when our spirit returns, awaiting its next adventure.

Loneliness and sadness are some of the most

debilitating conditions known to mankind. But what

if we could combat these terrible feelings through the

process of self-love? Our humanness disconnects us,

but as spirits, we have a constant connection with all

that is, and we are never truly alone.

Whilst it's a juggling act to manage our humanness and

stay in tune with spirit at the same time, the process

of loving ourselves allows us to embrace and truly

understand our own company. If you feel lost, then how

can you find anyone else if you must still find yourself?

Be complete. Love yourself. Find yourself, and others

will most certainly find you for that beautiful human

connection we all strive for.

When you are presented with stresses, disappointments, heartache, sadness, loss, and a whole range of other human emotions, an accompanying internal, intrusive chatter consumes you, preventing rest, peace, and love and, in many cases, creating isolation.

Have you ever wondered, really wondered, what might be happening when you experience turmoil like this? In those exact times, the Universe attempts to contact you, offer you teachings, and explain why the experiences present themselves.

When you feel low, sad, lost, disappointed, and disconnected, you function at a lower vibrational frequency. The Universe's energy functions at a higher frequency, making it difficult for you to tune in to its energy when in despair.

Try to remember this when presented with this chatter. Slow it down, and listen deeply to the Universe's gifted messages. Visualise a radio dial, and whilst breathing slowly and deeply, retune your connection, slowly moving the dial from the left to the right. Your station is there. Sometimes, it may have some crackle, but the more you tune in, the greater the signal will become. Not only during turmoil should his station be the channel you choose. Tune in every day, as all the love, peace, happiness, and prosperity exist here.

With love, gratitude, and hugs,

DJ Rod XXOO

We are angels sent to Earth embodied in a human form.
We have a tendency, however, to believe that we are
human first and that we either transcend to the spirit or
disappear completely once our human experience has
extinguished.

Our human form is like the gravitational pull that
prevents our spirits from soaring whilst we live our
physical existence. What happens when a bird lands in
an ocean that an oil spill has polluted? It can no longer
soar as it once did, and ultimately, it becomes stranded,
lost, and unable to survive, nor be as it was destined
to be.

We humans have become receptive to the belief that
we are stuck in that sludge and accept that we all must
endure the ravages of our humanity. What if we believed
that we are all gifted and all able to soar as our spirit
intended? We are all special and gifted, like the initial
intention of our creation.

Be the best you can, embrace your uniqueness
and special qualities, and don't let anyone tell you
otherwise. When you soar from the sludge, residuals
will always attempt to hold you back. Have strength,
courage, and resilience, and push through until you
soar as you were born to do.

By questioning your status, you risk losing your inner

peace and the beauty present right in this moment.

This is a time when you search for more and believe it

is something tangible and separate from yourself. On

closer observation, during these moments, you allow

your mind to wander free and lose your sense of the

importance of now. Generally, at this time, you catch

yourself in this place when you are not busy.

This gives you a perfect time to meditate or do

something else kind for your spirit. Go for a walk, go

out in nature, or drive to the beach. Here, the answers

and inspirations lie.

You light up the sky, sprinkling magic onto the Earth

where we stand, guiding us to the light that you

shine as a beacon from the stars. That conduit, like a

magnifying glass between the realms of heaven and

Earth, was gifted to you. An angel on Earth who has

returned to the source, you perform your role now. You

will not only leave a difficult-to-fill space but honour us

with the sparkle of the time you have shared with us.

For all of us, you have been a beautiful light, and

we know we can call on you whenever guidance or

inspiration beckons. When we stare into a bright light

and turn away and blink, the light still remains etched

on our retinas. This is how we can access you: by

closing our eyes, blinking a few times, and finding the

light, and we once again connect to the purity of your

love.

Blinking once, twice, and three times, you're here.

We at times feel that the weight of the world sits directly on our shoulders, weighing us down and restricting our ability to breathe or see the light. The depth of one's despair prevents clarity and locks one in a place of revolving grief. When one holds true to divinity, beauty constantly presents itself.

When one feels as if on the rainforest floor—deep down underneath the decaying matter, never seeing the light—one finds it difficult to see new life transforming. A seedling or a sapling grows deep within, awaiting its moment to peek through and meet the light. The decaying foliage, in fact, supplies the nutrients that assist one to grow. Wow! What a beautiful moment of transformative insight and shift.

So whenever you feel lost and narrate an inner belief of hopelessness, just reflect on the perfection and divinity that exist, and know that many opportunities continually present themselves for your healing.

Many of us sense that we lose pieces of ourselves whilst we allow others to dictate the terms of our existence and we generate a life of fortitude, but not one necessarily of pure purpose. If we're not mindful, our purpose can chip away, and negative self-beliefs and self-perceptions manifest themselves as the person we visualise in the mirror. We need to strip back the sediment that is the history of our lives and immerse ourselves back in the foundation of our perfection. Imagine we are Picasso paintings; that beauty and raw canvas exist as our core and our perfection—everyone unique, everyone beautiful.

We never lose pieces of ourselves, but through the process of our lives, we repaint and recolour our canvas, and now, we no longer have a resemblance of the perfect artwork that once existed. Allow yourself to locate that beautiful, raw, and unique Picasso again, like when someone finds an old painting at a garage sale or in an antique shop and the paint chips off, revealing a true Picasso underneath. We have given permission for others to paint over our canvas, but we have the ability to scrape off the paint for the purpose of finding our beauty, self-love, heart, passion, spirit, and happiness.

From one beautiful Painter to all you beautiful Picassos, I send my love and heart your way.

Rod XXOO

When viewing our lives we have a tendency to focus on the negatives and fears, and as a result fail to see the absolute beauty this is present everywhere we look. Look beyond fear and embrace the amazing gifts surrounding you.

Rod xx

Photo - Jenni Mac

Could the torture a being faces, with no evidence in his

or her current human manifestation, be the residual

effects of karma? Many of us wonder why certain

people, and sometimes ourselves, face complications

that have no reason to exist. Even when perfection sits

within our realm, we don't see the beauty in front of us,

and somehow, we manage to contribute to an outcome

that again provides for grief to reign supreme.

Forgiveness is available for all of us if we strive for

goodness and kindness and become servants of

humanity. We can unlock the shackles, providing a

passage to our ultimate learnings, and then return to

the source with the purity of our spirit intact. We are all

on our journey of discovery, but on our roads travelled,

we can bring love and goodwill to all that we have

contact with, even if it's just through a smile, a helping

hand, kindness, and understanding. We'll continue to

find our inner peace, purpose, and life goal of love,

happiness, and forgiveness.

When one misaligns with one's perfection and embarks
on a constant search for meaning, he or she has a
tendency to self-sabotage in an attempt to feel alive.
A fundamental exists in most things where one must
return to the essence to gather the perfect form
before reaching out and extending oneself when the
opportunity presents itself. What happens when you
fail to see the simplicity of returning to your core
(spirit) for realignment? Generally, you sustain an
injury or disease (physical, psychological, or spiritual)
where the Universe attempts to force you to slow
down, reflect, and recapture your truth. You fail to
grasp the perfection and continue down the path of
self-destruction.

Slow down, and tap into the love source. You'll find it
here, where all the beauty, happiness, and perfection
exist. This then manifests itself as self-love and the love
of all things, and if we all can find this enlightening
oasis—through meditation especially—the world
and the Universe will provide a more beautiful and
purposeful existence for all.

We possess boundless and abundant gifts. Our gifts, if
we choose to embrace them, are, in fact, our passions,
and if we manage to marry our many gifts and
passions, we will have truly magnificent lives. Close
your eyes for a moment, and acknowledge all the things
you're great at. In a blink, I know you have thought of
many, but another little voice pops up and challenges
that truth: "No, actually I'm not that good", "I can't
really do that", "I'm not as good as so-and-so", and
so on.

Whose voice is that—yours or one of a ghost from your
past? We each find ourselves at many stages; it is only
natural that others may appear better at some things,
but as a result of this, we talk ourselves down. We do
not measure up to another. However, we are beautiful
and perfect and exactly where we should be; that's why
we're here. Do as you do, and as you travel, embrace
your beauty, and play it forward. When from spirit and
heart, no fear exists.

It's a beautiful thing to accumulate knowledge and experiences. Gifts are offered to us as tools to realise our full potential, and through these pathways, we are presented with our truth. It may take a moment or a lifetime, or in some cases, when one is oblivious to his or her purpose and completely misses the true learnings, rebirth may be the solution.

Imagine this process as living our human experience in a circular motion, born and gathering until the final moment when the epiphany appears. Remember, it's not the accumulation that defines us. It's our heart and our love. Don't allow the ego to define the human sum of us.

Imagine we stand on top of a mountain at birth. On one side, we roll and experience our humanness only to return, hopefully, at the end of this journey enlightened and in the exact same place. But if we stay in tune with the heart and love, we can face the other way, and love is right there. This is ours, and we can accept that we were born already there, of purity, of love, and of divinity. As we accumulate a wealth of all experiences, our truth is to give back and assist others in reaching their truth, the one truth: love.

All things happen to prepare us for greatness. Have

you ever wondered why it seems that it never rains

but it pours? This space prepares us for the downpour

of success. Some may interpret these moments as

overwhelming, but these moments only overwhelm

us when we fail to prepare before these greater

opportunities present themselves. If we accept things

as perfect and continually reinforce our uniqueness

and connection to divinity, then we will constantly have

beneficial opportunities available to grasp. Be mindful,

be present, and be ready to accept the gifts. They're

ours for the taking; we just need to know that magic

exists with all of us.

All things will be exactly as they should be. A decision

will always arrive at its correct moment. Only retrospect

belies a belief in an alternative. At times, we all tend

to beat ourselves up about missed opportunities, and

as a result, we minimise ourselves, creating a negative

opinion of our self-worth. Be mindful of your self-talk,

and challenge the inner dialogue when speaking ill

toward the spirit.

When you pick this up, rephrase it as a positive learning

scenario, so only beautiful and positive messages

seep into your subconscious and spiritual depths. At

these points, you manifest true alignment, and peace,

happiness, and love become one with the spirit.

Can you remember the feeling of being in love when your heart races and your mind works in overdrive with thoughts about the next interaction? That feeling is, in fact, our spirit connecting with another spirit, interpreting it in human form for the purpose of acknowledging the beauty that exists when one connects with the universal consciousness. A perfect, pure connection occurs, but as humans, we don't always keep the arteries connected to the spirit healthy. We forget that to stay healthy, we must keep ourselves fit. Put goodness in for the greater return.

What happens if we don't treat our body with respect? We build unhealthy plaque and clog the connections that keep us well. Our spiritual arteries do not work too dissimilarly. Through healthy connections of love and kindness and acknowledging and respecting our human gift, we keep our heart, spirit, and love connections pure. That magnificent and amazing feeling of love can constantly have presence in your human form. Connect with the source, acknowledge the magic, and miracles will present you with feelings of love. Don't let plaque build in all facets of your life and restrict access to the purity of love.

Commencing any new experience starts with the first step. We tend to think of every step that we will have to navigate before we reach a goal, but thinking in such a way is debilitatingly overwhelming. Children have innocence and an inability to think beyond their first crawl, their first step, or their first run. But amazingly, we all meet these milestones.

When passion and purpose knock on your subconscious's door, do you let them in, or do you deadbolt them out and prevent them from ever entering your conscious thoughts due to your fears? Don't overthink; just do. Not unlike every other experience you've had that's led you to your greatness so far, the Universe will guide you, and you will summon energy when you take your first step.

Believe in yourself, and trust in divine guidance. Then success, happiness, love, passion, and prosperity will envelop your heart and spirit, and a life of purpose will manifest itself.

When the fog has settled and one has maintained the

higher ground of self-love and forgiveness, it manifests

a higher vibration and maintains a purity of existence.

It's so easy to allow ourselves to get caught in the fog,

battle our way through with hatred, and get bogged

down with the weight of it all. But if we choose this

option, then we will attract a continuing lower vibration,

and subsequent sadness and despair will become daily

and all-consuming friends.

Align with beauty. Align with love. Don't fight turmoil

with negativity, but shine love its way. Your heart and

spirit will lighten, and your path to happiness and love

will be light.

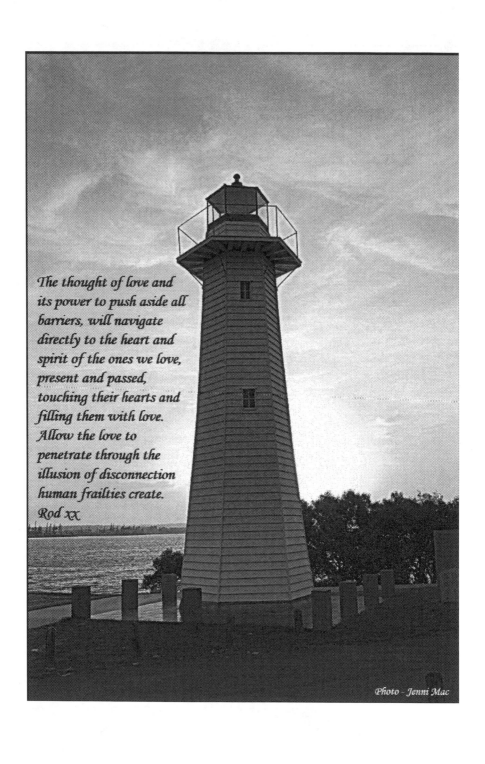

The thought of love and its power to push aside all barriers, will navigate directly to the heart and spirit of the ones we love, present and passed, touching their hearts and filling them with love. Allow the love to penetrate through the illusion of disconnection human frailties create.

Rod xx

Photo – Jenni Mac

Life is love; love is life. Love resonates as our core

ingredient, the spark that is our connection to our

divine self.

We mask our divinity with our self-perceptions and get

overtaken by our ego's belief that our human perception

is the only truth. Ego certainly has its place, but we

must keep in mind that it should not be our core belief.

Instead, ego is an encompassing element that makes

us human, something like an egg white, and our soul

and love are the yolk. If you ever struggle in human

form, retreat to your love space, as this will assist

you in finding meaning, inner peace, and happiness,

and ultimately, love will resonate back into the world.

Practise regularly, and greater understanding will

prevail.

We have a simple way to locate and maximise our

purpose and attract greater love into our existence. As

humans, we tend to lean toward negatives or what-ifs,

expecting to reach certain levels similar to others to

prove or validate our own self-worth. We can all access

abundance, but we measure abundance in so many

ways, and only we can determine what defines what

abundance looks like.

If we reflect for a moment or even meditate on giving

back during all our interactions, then we omit the

middleman—the ego—which measures our worth from

a human perspective. We have a direct link to the spirit,

and if we keep that in mind when reflecting on what we

do, then our measure is divine and guided by the spirit.

Truly, the purest of loves resonate and the ultimate

happiness are born here. Your purpose in a loving space

is to gift what is gifted to you for a greater, happier,

more loving, and more beautiful human experience.

Imagine your life and all the steps you've taken as

climbing a ladder to the highest mountain peak. We

all hope that every step continues to lead us to that

pinnacle. We do at times, however, have moments when

it feels we are backpedalling and going down that

ladder instead of up. We may view this as a negative

or some form of personal failure. But what if the

Universe is just guiding us down a few rungs so we see

a new perspective? We may find a ridge or hole in the

mountain that we can peer through to get a better view

of where we are going—a realignment of sorts due to a

wrong path pursued.

Never view this as a wrong or incorrect step but as a

guiding force realigning your path for greatness and

clarity, and in that moment, embrace the beauty that is

presented to you constantly. You just need to open your

heart to truly see it.

Why are we so unkind to ourselves? Would we speak

ill of a stranger walking down the street? We feel

comfortable with our internal self-talk, beating

ourselves up and being negative toward ourselves,

but congratulate others on their achievements. What

if we did that for ourselves? What if we were kind

to ourselves and congratulated ourselves instead of

finding fault?

Every motion and thought helps us realise the path

chosen, so why not make it a positive option? What if we

just tried to pull ourselves up when we caught ourselves

being unkind to ourselves? What if we changed the

narrative and reframed it as something positive?

Give it a try; you have nothing to lose. And as the old

saying goes, if you've got nothing nice to say, don't say

anything at all.

The Universe constantly evolves and presents new,

wonderful, and amazing insights as each spirit grasps

the next roller coaster of gifted events. In a spiral,

not unlike some kind of wormhole in the stars, as

we become more attuned to life, we get closer to the

needle tip of that spiralling wormhole. We experience

powerful angst at such moments, as we stand on the

cusp of the next wave of our universal and spiritual

journey. The anticipation of waiting for the next phase

can overwhelm us and create a need to go in reverse to

minimise this new awakening. The truth here and the

truth presented by the all-knowing guide us exactly the

way we should go. The opening of the next phase, after

squeezing through that needle tip, will be exactly like

the Big Bang. As humans, we experience pain, and our

ego will always endeavour to protect us, but as spirits,

we are already immune.

The culmination of all things guides us to the

destination that we're meant to travel to. Not unlike a

mule and a cart climbing Everest, we go through a tough

slog and much pain and heartache, but once we reach

the pinnacle, the view and experience are breathtaking.

Embrace it all.

Three truths exist: your truth, their truth, and the real

truth. We have a tendency, as physical beings, to get

caught up in others' truth and, as a result, minimise

our own truth. The real truth will always sit somewhere

in between, and provided our own truth is of purity

of action and intent, we can feel safe in knowing our

inner honour. We can never control another's truth or

how he or she may share that story with others. The

important lesson here is that it is none of our business,

and we shouldn't get caught allowing our thoughts

and subsequently our spirits to escape our grasp, as

this will feed any negativities or insecurities we might

possess.

Be strong, be whole, be pure, be of love, and honour

your heart and spirit.

Sometimes, some things just don't work the way

you'd like them to. That's the nature of humanity.

Acknowledging and appreciating this provides for

inner freedom and inner peace. The peace may not

come instantaneously, as again, humans require a

transformative period of reflection and recovery. Events

may not align, human interactions may not align, and

timings may not align. But for healing to occur, one

thing must happen: our hearts and minds must align.

The process of acknowledging and factoring in our

human foibles and reactions provides for our hearts'

equilibrium.

Reconnect, stay grounded, and be invigorated once

again by the source, your family, and amazing friends,

new and old. You have much to learn and so much

growing to do, especially seeing as you're such a little

fish in this glorious, universal ocean. Bathe in the

true essence of your own love for healing, growth, and

personal and spiritual self-discovery.

Focus on family.

Focus on friendships.

Focus on happiness.

Focus on kindness.

Focus on forgiveness.

Focus on peace.

Focus on love.

Focus on gratitude.

Love,

Rod XXOO

To serve is our mission. When self-worth wholly

consumes people, they will forever be slaves to the

existence that they forge for themselves. This is not to

say that this approach is undeserving, as we all deserve

success and the accompanying rewards that encompass

such an existence. But when their purpose and

existence extend beyond themselves for the benefits of

all mankind, it presents the greatest rewards, and a life

of true happiness, and ultimate love will prevail.

Instant gratification seems enticing in many varied

forms. As beautiful as it may appear in the moment, one

must acknowledge the varying aspects of this ideology.

There is the spiritually aligned mindfulness aspect, and

there is the physically aligned human side, where one

may immerse oneself for the sake of his or her human

deficiencies.

To stay true to one's human existence and authentic in

one's life's path, the physical and spiritual aspects of

life require alignment. Not all experiences immediately

present themselves as beautiful; however, in time, when

one reaches alignment, the beauty will unfold, and one

will embrace all interactions throughout as love for the

purpose of all of life's experiences.

Beauty is in the eye of the beholder. In reading that, one

may first conclude that physical appeal supersedes all

other beautiful attributes one might possess. If we delve

deeply into the spirit and view ourselves from our heart

and our mind's eye, then we will truly see the beauty of

our soul.

Look deep within, and connect with your beauty at a

universal level.

What is truth? Truth is an interpretation of what one's

lifelong experiences, beliefs, morals, and values have

forged, and it is infinite from its birth and only of

purity for the one who owns it. No one truly has the

capacity to read another's mind to determine what truly

lies within. The truthsayer resides with one's inner

beliefs and convictions. Our truth is ours and cannot

be judged or determined by another's belief, just as

we cannot judged others'. If an untruth is presented as

truth for the purposes of manipulation or deception,

then the owner of that mistruth will have an internal

struggle and grief until clarity of conviction (truth) and

ultimate internal peace prevail. If kindness and love are

the foundation of one's truth, even though pain may

very well be a component, then the path one leads will

head for purpose and purity of intent.

Memories are gifts provided to us through the accumulation of experiences. Within these memories exist our learnings and growths. The people we shared these experiences with are, in fact, our greatest teachers throughout the shared period. We can maintain some memories, when experienced with another, over a lifetime, and others for a shorter period, but neither holds lesser or greater importance. All memories are presented at the exact right time for all parties to shift them to a higher vibrational plain of existence, if we embrace the lessons in such a way.

The arteries of our intertwining lives provide parallel alignment for a time, where beauty presents itself for us to embrace it and internally immerse ourselves in it for the purpose of embracing our inner understandings. Our journeys can zigzag over a road map and eventuate at the same destination, or they could at some stage change directions, and we can call on our memory for inspiration.

Within all that makes us human, our experiences, our learnings, and ultimately our memories are our toolbox. Think of it like this: the greater the experiences, the bigger the toolbox. If one has had to struggle, his or her toolbox might look like Kennards Hire, and if this is the case, then he or she might share the accumulated tools with others to assist them in repairing what's happening for them.

We have a beautiful opportunity to give back and feel inspired and connected all at the same time.

A life of hurt, searching for the truth—what is the meaning of it all?

Coloured with beauty sprinkled throughout, there is only one constant,

and that constant is love. In a life of truth searching for love, people come in, and people

fall out. Our families grow old and kids grow up. There is only one constant,

and that constant is love.

What do we have that we all have to hold—a consistent that is love and also all things?

A consistent that we all strive for—love! Hold on, and strive for the beauty that we are all

deserving of: the consistency of love.

Flowing through us all is love. Connecting all our hearts is love.

Our human interactions are defined by love. We all strive to be safe in love.

Follow your heart's path to love. And when the final bow is done

and the show is going off the road, look back, and acknowledge the beauty.

I guarantee there's only one purity, and that's the truth of love and all it encompasses.

With love and heart,

Rod XXOO

The condition of humanity is connectedness. Our whole primal existence involves seeking out love and finding that person we can share our experiences with. This person does not complete us, as we have already perfected completion, and we appreciate our uniqueness and connection to all. These other unique beings ideally are an ingredient in our greatness on Earth, where human happiness and human love connect. In this connection, one finds solace in his or her achievements and celebrations. All humans venture into their journey and look at their memories as their inspiration.

This does not suggest that a solo existence doesn't provide for great achievements. Quite the contrary. Independently, an individual can achieve wonderful human outcomes—wealth, fame, and a multitude of other measurable things. But does this truly provide for the completeness of the connection and magic of love? With love, we find true greatness, and with love, we can truly appreciate greatness. Find that balance, and the greatness of love and the greatness of success will taste so much sweeter.

Ah, the nectar of the Universe: love!

Rod XXOO

Mysteries exist! We can either be debilitated by them

or mesmerised by them. Which option sounds more

enticing? We have a tendency to lean toward the

unknown with fear and ultimately become reactive

vessels, awaiting change, and in retrospect, we always

make it through. But what if we embraced the mystery

and were the driver, proactive in our existence and

inspired and excited by what's to appear? How exciting

is it to be alive (and lovin' it!)?

Sending love and mystery in your direction,

Rod XXOO

Love is not to understand; love is to trust. The

dimension of love is immeasurable, beyond our realm

and capacity to truly appreciate. Love is the bond—

the glue that holds everything together. Love is the

conduit between hearts and souls, the physical and the

spiritual.

Why do so many atrocities exist in the name of love?

Could it be, as humans, we fear the immeasurable or

the loss of control that could happen if we just trusted

the magical existence of love? The ego is the physical.

A measure of self is expected here, and love is of pure

spirit.

Love is everywhere; we just need to open our hearts

and let it in for our healing and ultimately the world's

healing.

No individual is immune to the conditioning of humanity. We all must go through the struggles when presented to us and find our path and truth within the turmoil until we reach the other side. Rest assured we will reach the other side; that is the guaranteed truth, if we allow healing to flow through us and to be accessed by the source and purity of love.

Many of us hold on to grief because of either guilt or a belief that by letting go, we will no longer have a purpose or identify as complete or part of something that once was. These self-defeating beliefs and habits only exist for the person holding on, and ultimately, that person becomes his or her self-identified persona, limiting healing, future opportunities, and monumental possibilities.

Let go, reconnect with friends, and be kind, forgiving, and respectful to the spirit within. Look in the mirror, and tell yourself how beautiful you are. Acknowledge that with all past experiences, good and bad, we only had the capacity to deal with them the exact way we did, as that is exactly all we had. Start a daily ritual of looking deep into your own eyes, saying something kind, and acknowledging your beauty. These things sink into your subconscious and assist you in becoming aligned with self-love, self-respect, and self-forgiveness.

Our human experience is not unlike a cocoon, all

unique and beautiful in the eyes of the divine. But it's

up to us to keep this vessel in check and safe whilst

developing and transitioning through until we blossom

back to the spirit.

What is our truth? When we look deep inside ourselves, what do we see? If we listen to our internal voice—the one our experiences of inadequacy and unworthiness guide, the one that haunts us from our humanity— we may very well see a flawed individual incapable of being anything more than what we present at this exact moment. Without us ever realising it, an even greater depth of self-knowing exists, only accessible through clarity of thought and purity of intention. Our humanness clutters our thoughts, but we are more than our human experience alone. We are enlightened and born of light and love.

How do we locate this depth of clarity and connect with the source? We need to quiet our minds and thoughts and give them permission to access our truth where we derived from it as a spirit. Even if you read this without the quiet, your truth is right there with you and telling you that you are a gift of beauty and love. However, before you reinforce it, clutter appears, and you get bogged down in your humanness and the ultimate daily grind.

Give yourself the gift of quiet reflection, self-love, and nurturing. Then the truth will reveal itself and solidify your self-awareness and daily existence. Love and happiness are derived from here and provide guidance to all the beauty and connections we are here to experience and ultimately share and guide.

We all place so many expectations and rules upon

ourselves that we often minimise the now. Internal

grief manifests itself as a result, generally due to old

wounds from childhood or other significant moments

in our lives. When we get caught up in this negative self-

belief, we can feel like frauds and ultimately unworthy

in the eyes of others. In meditation, reflect on this

exact notion. The only truth is the now and the purity

of love. If love acts as the foundation of oneself and

all the relationships one has connections to, and we

embrace that beauty and gift in the now, then all other

expectations or future occurrences will find their way

at the exactly right time.

The time has come to not overthink and to embrace the

love, as love is just that: perfection.

Love, in its simplest form, means having a heart full of appreciation and gratitude, feeling safe and nurtured, without a concern that things will fall around our feet. We all deserve these beautiful sentiments, and this condition is rightfully ours. But what conditions exist that make these sometimes insurmountable or unachievable? Our inner belief does. Our inner belief says we are not worthy due to a conditioning process of our past. If we reflect for a moment on where we are in our development, we see we hold on to such flawed belief systems. We can truly see that we've never had the capacity to own or define ourselves due to this. We continually give our power away to a time that no longer exists. We constantly seek love and believe in its true essence, and we think someone else should provide our own worth, only to know someone else originally took it away, and this pattern continues throughout our lives of never feeling worthy of love.

We must open our hearts and let forgiveness in. We must take our power back and acknowledge the journey we all have faced—some truly difficult and some not so. But one thing remains true: we define our own truth, we determine our worth, we deserve love, and we must embrace the presented challenges and learnings that give us strength. Love your life, and embrace every moment that has been presented to you. It's not always easy to see whilst in the storm, but every storm eventually changes directions, especially if you navigate to your own destination through divine guidance.

We find our love within; that is where our essence

exists. We access our own love in our reservoir where

we share our love for others. Self-love fills us, and

external love complements it but can never exhaust.

Appreciation and gratitude exist in this sacred place,

where safety and inner nurturing go hand in hand

and where our foundation can never rock. Passion and

forgiveness exist here as a sanctuary of our soul and

spirit. Go within and find your reservoir; it exists in all

of us, and we all deserve this beauty.

I truly and deeply send my love to you to complement

your growing river of love that exists within us all. Feel

the beauty radiate.

Wow!

Vulnerabilities exist in all of us, and our hearts constantly seek out avenues to minimise such potentially debilitating qualities. We tend to gravitate toward an isolated element and hold on to it to maintain safety; that's just the nature of humanity. However, when we cannot access this one element, we may find our ability to hold steadfast diminished.

Connections and linkages are an extremely important factor in minimising the control this one isolating philosophy has. By restricting our initial desire to connect with one element for safety and not allowing all eggs to go in one basket, we can minimise the spiralling effect and provide diversity and exposure to other extremely important lessons. It's important to not minimise and to truly embrace the beauty of all our individual connections, but as a collective, no one will ever have the capacity to go in isolation.

Not unlike the sun setting at dusk, the light of ones lifeforce can never be diminished. It will rise again to shine a beacon of magic, guiding your way. Follow your dreams and constantly await your light to shine, as it most certainly will, if you only believe. Rod xx

A physical trauma to the body may meet a doctor's orders of no strenuous activity for six weeks for healing to take place. However, the healing time of emotional pain is more difficult to measure, similar in that one must not go through more trauma until one regains a certain level of peace. Otherwise, the healing will slow, and the trauma will escalate. Would you go play a contact sport in the six weeks whilst your fracture heals? The same goes for distancing yourself and putting in place strategies that assist in healing the emotional, psychological, and spiritual ache that exists at your core.

Minimise the things that reawaken toxins. Stop being a detective. Stop seeking out information that only leads to greater heartache. Stop thinking about the what-ifs, and stop borrowing stress from the future. Own your heart, and don't look for reasons why. Only look for reasons to move forward, and love and embrace the opportunity presented.

You have so much beauty ahead, as well as the beauty that exists now. Love in the moment—not in the past, not in the future. Love the people—your family and friends—who love you, and send love out into the world; it will come back and generate an abundance of peace and happiness. Remember we determine our happiness—no one else.

We give love unconditionally, as this element resonates

within and is gifted from our maker, from where we

once came, and to where we will all return again. We, as

humans, however, can easily get caught up in our heads,

and when love does not get reciprocated, we place it

on ourselves to feel inadequate or unworthy of love in

return. We ask the questions, "What did I do wrong?"

and "Why am I not worthy of love?"

Our ego poses these questions, and our ego attempts

to defeat our truth and purity of spirit. What if we

asked ourselves when presented with another's

nonreciprocating love, "If our love is gifted to another

but refused, then who does that love belong to?" Think

about it for a moment. Intimacy works for us and feeds

our souls with our self-worth and self-love. Before we

can truly love another, we must truly love ourselves.

Scholars and healers have said that there are no mistakes and all that presents itself is perfect in its make-up. But why does perfection hurt so much? In attempting to understand the true message that comes from this approach, one can only surmise our potential and purpose are of a higher order. Remaining in the state that we find ourselves in does not provide the greater good and does not align with our true gift of giving. We are not always privy specifically to our role; however, if we lose sight or go off track, we may find that we are steered correctly through some form of challenge or struggle. After we are alerted through a painful realisation that is forced on us, we must clarify our gifts to give and do more for the greater good for mankind.

Within your grief and struggles is a message. Listen carefully to its meaning and direction. Here, your motivation and purpose exist. Grab a hold, and follow the messages gifted to you, for they will guide and align with your greater contributions on Earth. I'm listening and hearing the greater good I can do and achieve.

We can become addicted to the nature of suffering
and grief. Immersion in suffering triggers the reward
centre of the brain, contributing to the release of the
brain chemical cortisol. The longer we remain in a state
of suffering, the greater the addiction can potentially
become. The amygdala, which signals fear to your body,
goes into overdrive with the release of cortisol, making
it difficult to centre your emotions or regulate them
as you would have before the trauma (Bartel, 2013).
If we do not control grief and are not mindful of the
effects of cortisol, then we can easily self-sabotage so
that we continue to access this naturally occurring
drug. It definitely has its place in healing, but over
time, if we continually access it due to a wandering
and uncontrolled mind, then addiction and other
physiological changes may present themselves.

Be mindful, meditate, give and receive love,
communicate, eat well, exercise, immerse yourself
in your passion, and sleep. These wonderful healing
strategies help us all through our struggles.

A little breath, as innocent as it may appear, holds many

of the Universe's secrets. It is the only true universal

gift, apart from our spirit, that connects us completely

in our physical form. An accepted breath has been

accepted by millions of other inhabitants over millions

of years in potentially millions of galaxies. Imagine

that for a moment. Each breath out connects to the next

person who breathes components of your breath in; who

breathes out, connecting to nature; and who releases

it again for another species to breathe in again. And

the cycle continues. When fraught with the elements of

unhappiness or distress, think about your breath. Take

it slowly in, and accept its radiance. Accept its healing,

and accept its wisdom and knowledge. It may seem like

a simple breath to some, but it is so much more. It is

universal life, and we unknowingly have access to its

beauty and healing power. I send you my breath and

healing messages that I've learned on my journey of

discovery.

Love and light. *Breathe.*

The ego is a sensitive element to our existence and a component that seeks to own and control our thoughts and perceptions. The ego holds you and keeps you stuck for the fear and belief of failure. The ego would prefer to have you believe that you're intact and guide you to believe you are righteous and on the higher plain. But truth be known the ego hopes to achieve exactly this in actual fact. It has no capacity to allow for light and spirit. It can't see the learnings, growth, and solutions present. We remain in some moments for far too long; sometimes, it's true we do still need to have more learnings in that place, but more often than not, the ego's hold on our fear keeps us still.

The beautiful moments and the beautiful people we have shared a lifetime with will never leave our side, as they are the frames that helped erect the spiritual mansion we have today. They exist beneath the gyprock; within the walls, floors and ceilings of our lives. Without their input and assistance in our structure, we may very well have collapsed. The outside world doesn't see these experiences and previous loves and supports one has had in life, but they are there. You might paint over your experiences and give them new colour and life, but they still sit safely beneath your presenting existence.

Control your ego, and accept your learnings. Don't be afraid to let go, especially when you need to cover an old wall with a fresh coat of paint to freshen up an old experience or learning. Truly think about whether remaining where you presently are has a benefit or purpose, and if you know your ego is what has caused you to stay, let it go. Give it your blessing; it will be difficult, no doubt, as change such as this is difficult for all physically, and the heart will feel the pain. Call the pain *love, learning, gratitude, respect, forgiveness,* or *beautiful,* breathe; relax; and let go. It will turn out just perfect and the way it is meant to be. Through heartache and pain, the greatest learnings occur.

A self-enquiring prophecy results from an inner belief system that resonates with one's true purpose. We come from many places and experiences. These moments lay the foundation for our future self-awareness. Here lies the potential complication. You may come from an experience where the foundation is solid and you reach for something obtainable and expected, or you may rise from a foundation that many years of turmoil have impacted, and as a result, this assists in defining your existence as flawed or unobtainable.

Feeling unloved or unworthy will result in an enduring existence of just that. We will inevitably self-sabotage at a subconscious level; that is how it must be. And when we find love, we will always fear that true love is unachievable and act in a self-defeating way.

We will, however, find a moment of clarity where we need to name and heal this conditioning. From this moment of clarity and enlightenment, healing begins. Struggles are to be had for the greater purpose of inner growth and spiritual awareness.

Name your demons, and own them. No longer allow them to have power over you. Take your power back, and love yourself unconditionally. Be mindful of your self-perception, and be kind to yourself.

How do we achieve true happiness? Happiness is
the fulfilment of a life well lived. Happiness is the
appreciation of all things beautiful, especially the
beautiful people you have in your inner circle. This
consists of family, close friends, work colleagues, and
the transient souls you welcome into your life when
it requires additional learnings and challenges. A
truth of knowing is not easily identifiable, as we get
caught up in our everyday struggles and attempts to
present to the world how the world expects us to be.
The commercial world doesn't want us to find peace. It
needs and requires us to be frantic slaves to continuing
hypnotic selling and the feeding of our ego in an
attempt for greed to rule supreme. Get back in touch
with your inner knowing, connect with nature, embrace
the beauty that surrounds us, be grateful, find love, and
appreciate the goodness and connectedness that pure
love brings.

Be passionate about those things that you love, and
allow others to love you back. Forgive yourself and truly
love yourself and know that you are loved, because I
love you!

Rod XXOO

Peculiarity is, in essence, the component of one's individual existence that sets one apart from other humans. This unique trait formulates one's destiny and the path one must travel for one's life purpose, happiness, and ultimate success. It is of utmost truth that others pursuing varied paths will not have the capacity to appreciate another's aligned destiny and ultimate path and may very well criticise the path to either maximise his or her own self-worth (ego) or hover at a lower vibrational level. To truly understand the alignment, one must generate balance, truth, and ultimate and intimate appreciation of universal gifts.

Stay true to your inner knowledge. Listen carefully to yourself from within, as here, truth and connectedness align. Here, we meet our maker. Here, we are guided to our truth. Do not align with the mistruths of others and their inability to seek and align with their own truth, resulting in attempts to bring you down, as they are also where they need to be in relation to their own level of growth.

Be who you're meant to be—beautiful, unique, truthful, loving, and on your path to your happiness.

It's amazing the connectedness we share. When support
and love are called upon, amazing friends pop up and
provide a helping hand to prop you up. Each and every
one of us has experienced a plethora of amazing and
unique experiences, and in some cases, we may never
get the chance to share our insights and wisdom until a
hand is raised and support required.

Truly reflect for a moment, and think about if and
when someone needs a helping hand. An understanding
shoulder can work wonders in lifting that person into
a different phase of self-perception at that moment.
This support can act as a deciding factor in the
commencement of their own healing, and from this
sharing, your own growth, development, and healing
commence. The more you give, the more you share; the
more you love, the greater happiness, love, and peace
you will discover, and this will then be synonymous
with your truth and inner existence.

"I know it's there, but I'm too scared to see it." Many

of us have this exact fear when it comes to connecting

to our spirit. I believe we all know this deep in our

spiritual core, driving our human vehicle, but we get

stuck in this vehicle, not unlike a seat-belt latch, not

wanting to disengage. The two components of spirit and

vehicle meld into one, as the spirit is like a fluid and

can become whatever we desire it to be. However, due to

our fear, we choose to be more human, and we lose our

inner awareness and truth of existence. As we lie awake

quietly at night, listening to our own breath, we have

the sense of something more than the physical that we

shy away from, and we disregard it as our imagination.

We can't bear exposure to our true lineage, as the fears

and traumas from our past prevent our reconnection.

Meditate on this, and find the clarity within the waves

and windows of connectedness.

Why pain? As confusing as pain is, it's the catalyst of

change. We must have a trigger for our awakening,

and any other emotion generally will not allow us

to connect. If things are perfect and smooth sailing,

we will go on through our lives blissfully unaware.

Pain enlightens our path; through pain, our greatest

growth and connectedness occur. Pain is our conduit

to the Universe. In history, as tragic as it may appear,

the greatest events involving humanity have led to

our greatest growth. However, history also magnifies

the imbalance of our existence as spirits and creates

a belief that humans in themselves have all the power

to act and make decisions without true guidance or

spiritual purpose, and this has led to where we are

today. In spite of personal pain, small wins provide

connectedness, giving us purpose and clarity.

Open your heart, and let guidance and love in. Let them

show you your path, and in time, healing and a new

way—a better way—will emerge.

The simplicity of a higher purpose is an easy thing

to articulate; however, in the midst of uncertainty,

confusion can quite simply eradicate the foundation

of the truth we once held dear and close to our hearts.

Breathe through this, and affirm that through your

intuition and inner knowing, love will always be part of

the greater plan.

Richard Bach wrote in his 1970 novel *Jonathan*

Livingston Seagull, "If you love someone, set them free.

If they come back they're yours; if they don't they never

were." I think it's important to acknowledge this quote;

however, I think when one loves oneself, that person

needs to consider taking control and setting him- or

herself free, instead of the other entity. One shouldn't

treat oneself so unkindly and wait until another makes

a decision while one waits in the wings, possibly for

ultimate heartache (just a thought and reflection on

self-love).

Don't mistake current complications for part of

previous life challenges. They are separate, independent

moments, each one worked through at its own pace.

Most people face the problem of merging the past

and present, and this, in turn, swells all current and

previous life challenges as one whole tragedy that is

difficult to overcome. Consider this mantra: "Zone and

own." Zone the complication. Own the complication.

Don't mix the complication. This way, you can work on

it more easily. Complications and challenges don't all

belong together.

In the stillness where patience lives, true beauty
echoes out for all to see and hear. One cannot hear the
magic where the clutter is deafening. Rod xx

Photo - Jenni Mac

The universal consciousness is like an ocean, or a balloon filled with air. If you don't disturb it, its inhabitants will continually go about their blissful and peaceful existence, interacting with all in a nonlinear alignment. But when someone accesses this abundant source of all knowing—a bit like when a pin pierces the balloon or a plug is pulled from a bath—the purity pours out. Visualise how that will release to give you all that you need. How do we as physical beings create that pin or pull that plug? We can meditate and again ask the question, even without having any idea of what to expect or the desired outcome. Give in to the source, and give permission for the source to access you.

You only need to have awareness of the signs of this. The lessons and answers will present themselves as intuition, a sixth sense. They may present themselves not as answers in a human form but subtler than that. This is the skill. Be open to it, and feel the message coming through. In the silence, we are most at one with the source. Try not to fill the gap with noise, as it will blur and interfere with the connection, a bit like a conference call, with everyone talking.

How will you ever get clarity?

Locating your passion gets you out of bed in the

morning and provides you with the motivation to want

to chase it constantly. Talking about wealth factoring

into this approach to life, this approach will provide

abundance—the abundance to live every day and find

that sole soul purpose. We provide this love, respect,

and support to our family and friends and the external

people we serve, but this passion gives back so much,

and the return of wealth can then filter back into the

greater world. There's no need for second-guessing or

uncertainty. Immerse yourself in the chosen purpose

of this physical existence. Find this happiness, find this

greatness, and locate the thing you are the best in. That

will serve the world. That is what's it all about.

Every moment of our present is due to the accumulation of our life events until now. Consider for a moment what makes you happy, and acknowledge to yourself these are your gifts. You can accept and embrace this feeling at every instance. We own this, as do all of us.

When we step back into the past and drag our early life experiences into the present, we can find ourselves consumed with the pain and suffering these previous experiences presented to us. Again, if we acknowledge that these experiences moulded us, we can navigate our happiness for today and then let the experiences rest and remain in the past, never to haunt us in the present. This is the meaning of forgiving the past and moving on to live in the present moment. We can do this for ourselves and for the ones we love.

Love, embrace, forgive, and be present. These are the ingredients.

Your heart, when giving to others, needs to give love

only. Your heart will attract exactly what it gives

out. If your heart is broken and you're impacted by a

disturbance in your existence, and if you send out your

heart's energy with disturbance, you'll attract that back.

Imagine your heart sending out energy like an arm

covered with honey. Sending out pure love will attract

and stick to pure love on the return home, when the

pure love returns safely within. However, if you send

out love with anger, hatred, sadness, despair, and the

like, then these will stick on your return and contribute

to your already-unbalanced and misaligned state. Take

a moment before responding. Take a breath, and contain

and work on your inner understanding when dealing

with turmoil. This is exactly what you have control

of—not others' views, opinions, and ways of existence.

When you feel ready, send forgiveness, love, and purity

of thought and action; this will attract to you all the

goodness and magic that exist.

Attachments are cruxes that hold us in a pattern of self-despair and discouragement. They make us think we need to cling relationships as paramount to the healing and ultimate completion of a life journey. Some find a truth and make a decision appropriate to rectify it, and some feel shaken until they have an epiphany. However, some just continue down the road to maturation, never truly realising their greater potential. Listen to your heart, and know that acceptance of a lesser life is not your calling. All deserve happiness and love. Such a transformation will be difficult, but if another person keeps you downtrodden, is the relationship really healthy?

Own your heart, and speak your truth, and if another does not contribute to your greatness, then it's time to think about your beauty within and rightful access to your heart's purpose.

Clarity appears when one has the opportunity to reflect

on all things beautiful. No matter the situation one

encounters, the only truth that resonates as purity

is that of love and happiness. As humans, we have

moments that require a dance, when compromise

is part of the equation; that goes without saying.

However, when happiness is fleeting and only appears

momentarily, do we stay true to our hearts and at one

with the essence of self-love and self-respect? Reflect

on your unique beauty and deserved rights of love and

happiness. Stay true to yourself, communicate, and

make modifications for the purpose of gaining your

power and inner strength back. It is only through self-

advocacy and self-love that others can appreciate your

honour. Don't give your power away, as that enables

others to treat you with disrespect.

You know what to do.

The depth of one's heart is limitless, as is the depth that comes when one truly appreciates and acknowledges the magnitude of love, creates a bridge between the dimensions, and connects the heart directly to our source. Within this realm, one touches the purity of a connection, both physically and spiritually, and enmeshes all the senses for the purpose of pure alignment. As human beings, we allow ourselves to get stuck in the physicality of this current journey, preventing connections to our truth and rightful place for accessing the beauty that exists for us all to embrace. Through love and connection, and letting go of our human expectations and limited beliefs of the beauty of our true existence, we can again connect to the perfection that exists for us all. Through love, we find our way, as love is the key that unlocks our blocks and opens our doors to the magic Universe that awaits us all.

Embrace all love, and unlock the happiness that is gifted to us, as love creates love and generates the ripples that connect us all and allow our hearts to get gently pushed in the direction of greater love.

We are flawed in the eyes of others, just as we see the flaws in others ourselves. These are just the natural foibles of humanity. But when identifying the truth of happiness and connections and factoring in not only ours but others' flaws, what main condition do we all strive for, deserve, and long for? Happiness and love are indeed two of the main elements we are entitled to.

In identifying happiness and love within oneself and others and acknowledging flaws (and love is the key element and the flaws insignificant), we give up the opportunity for love and happiness and continue our journey of self-loving but independent agents. Or we connect and together find the truth of love and happiness and work through it as part of our continuing journey of discovery. Flaws exist inevitably, but if the conditions for love, mutual respect, kindness, and happiness exist, then we need to direct our energy and focus here, not toward insignificant elements that exist in all. Don't miss your opportunity for connection and love. Take the risk, and feel alive.

I finally see the clarity of my part, my sabotage, and my

fear of losing myself and immersing myself in another

for the purpose of what I believed to be the truth of

love. People shared the importance of individuality with

me many times, and I even preached this myself, but

it appears I had no real concept of its true meaning. I

truly believed that to love someone deeply was to invest

my whole existence in making that person as happy as I

could. The truth is we can only find and manifest such

love by loving ourselves, and others of similar value

and existence gravitate toward that kind of love. Two

lights meet and illuminate the same path. Together and

with the support of other enlightened beings, shine

love onto the world and out into the Universe. Your light

is welcome at that line, but your physical and human

presence must remain outside. This is the truth of

healthy human and spiritual interactions.

As dusk falls upon us and the earth commences its daily healing ritual, it puts on a beautiful and dazzling display of magic for us all to experience. Don't destroy, only protect and nurture the magic gifted to us. Rod xx

Photo - Jenni Mac

Humans endure. That's just what we do! We can

never truly appreciate our strength and resilience

until something calls upon them. We can only hope

that we treat each other with love, kindness, mutual

respect, understanding, and tolerance, but the acts

of others are out of our control, so we must face,

accept, acknowledge, and endure these acts and the

accompanying struggles and move forward. Through

forgiveness and the continuation of our inner growth

and connection to our aligning force and true direction,

we will gain the strength and resolve to continue.

Only through pain can inspirations and a new way of

being be born. And only a forgiving heart can manifest

true peace within. To fester means to decay; to forgive

means to live. Reconciliation is not necessary; however,

it is important that you don't carry the weight and you

have forgiveness in your heart.

We only ever have one pure truth: the truth of

ourselves. We can only ever have purity of belief and

connection when we are attached to the source—the

source being us, connected as one with all that is.

Physical truths separate from ourselves have their own

value and measure we can never truly know, as only

those entities have their specific truth and value set.

Nonetheless, humanness requires connection, but also

of extreme importance is that one's inner truth remains

infinite, aligned, and not measured by another's

physical interpretation of the importance of his or her

own existence. The key to purity is one's pure love of

oneself and pure love and connection to God.

Love with all your heart, but make sure you protect the

inner sanctum with self-love and universal love, not

physical love alone, as this ingredient can break one's

heart.

We need to protect our core and not allow the physical

realm to reach this inner and pure component of our

physical existence. This place is designated only for the

spirit; it is our master key that opens the door to our

next reality. We can't contaminate this sacred place with

codependency or attachment to the physical realm.

How we think is how we feel. What we think is what we are. Be mindful of the words you choose when referring to yourself, as any and all negativities sink in, and the subconscious mind listens closely. The same thing applies to flattering things you say about yourself.

Listen closely. Pull yourself up on anything negative, and change it to a positive. Don't think about it; just do it. With kindness and self-love, you will find yourself happier, more content, grateful, loving, peaceful, and confident. The energy you disperse attracts energy in return, not unlike how stamina builds for the spirit.

I'm sending everyone a little reminder to be kind to yourself and love all that you are, because I do.

Rod XXOO

Imagine your whole human experience to be like an hourglass. You're born pure, and the top half of your glass is filled with sand; that's your consciousness. As you experience life, you start to identify with who you are, and as sand flows to the lower part of your hourglass, this becomes your subconscious—the self-identifying components that become your belief system. If you continually allow negativity to infiltrate the sand at the top, then negativity becomes your default point, inner belief, and self-identifying image. But are we born this way? I hear you answer, "No!"

We are born pure. True, throughout our development, others' opinions and negative experiences tarnish us, but do we truly need to define ourselves by others' opinions or difficult experiences? No way! We can reprogram; just turn your hourglass over, and start refilling your conscience with positive self-talk, self-belief, and self-love. This then drifts into our subconscious and becomes our belief system. Write down some beautiful affirmations about yourself, and post them in strategic places around your home. Read them to yourself. Visualise them, and the magic will commence.

A woman presented herself as problem saturated. She carried around everything that could possibly be wrong. The enormity of what she carried weighed her down, and she had been carrying this weight for as long as she could recall. As she shared every facet of her life, flicking from one dilemma to another, she stirred all the complications in a cauldron. As each problem bubbled in the cauldron, that became her immediate focus, but the cycle of all her concerns continued.

In realising this, the cauldron turned into a twister, reaching far and wide, past, present, and future. This twister was monstrous, picking up future problems that didn't and more than likely never would exist, and past problems that were no longer relevant. A twister picks up houses, cars, and even cows, and this is a lot like how her life sucked in potential problems that didn't exist but were in her peripheral sphere.

She borrowed stress from the future and her past and carried it on her shoulders in the present. She was so weighed down that she couldn't move forward. But then one moment, she understood that she needed to slow down and stop the twister, create calm, stop sucking in problems far and wide, and focus on her wellness in the present moment.

When one thinks from one's head-mind, he or she can

overanalyse and miss the opportunity to experience life

from the heart space, or passion place. Fear exists in

the mind, and it prevents us from becoming more than

we truly can be. Go within and feel and find your truth.

Don't confuse it with what others might measure as

success. Find your own beauty and the things that you

truly love, and all things beyond comprehension will

appear.

All actions have reactions. And all experiments and

experiences determine one's path. We only have control

over ourselves, and if we maintain purity of all actions,

purity of existence will manifest itself.

When one gets thrown about with the turmoil of life,

it gets extremely difficult to see a clear path of hope,

clarity, and opportunity. It resembles the feeling of

getting thrown around after being dumped in the

surf, all disoriented and not knowing which way is up.

However, more often than not, we find the surface, take

a breath, and swim to shore, or even go in for some

more dumpings. Do we ever learn? Indeed, we do, as

our learnings are continuous, and sometimes, we need

to reinforce the experience to grasp the actual learning

presented. Some things appear insurmountable. But if

we rephrase it as *in-sur-mount-able*, then we are *able*

to *mount* and ride any challenge or wave that we are

presented with.

A woman dealing with multiple experiences of grief and loss couldn't find peace and kept falling back into despair. Like a dissected image of the Earth, her trauma and pockets of traumatic experiences appeared as cracks that seemed to lead to the surface. She continually tripped on these cracks that constantly reminded her of her grief and ultimate sadness. She explored ways she could reduce her trips over these constant reminders of her painful past, and she articulated that with a new, smooth road laid—for example, with concrete—she wouldn't have as many trip-ups. She meditated on how she might achieve this and eliminate revisiting her ongoing grief.

She changed her patterns, had new experiences, got out and met new people, and the list went on.

We are all born with the same canvas as everyone else,

and we colour our canvases at different stages with

different colours. The people we meet help us chose

our colours; some experiences are great and positive

and others not. Through the colouring of our lives, we

have moments of dark and moments of light, and again

have the capacity to select the beauty within all our

experiences. Ultimately, after all our physical lessons

and colours have blended, we are all left with the same

coloured canvas. We might have differences in the

beginning and transition to our next phase, but the

beginning and the transition are our true connection.

Let's attempt to have this true connection in the middle

also.

If we viewed our relationships from space, visualising our interactions with our loved ones like a jigsaw puzzle, we would see that one straight line doesn't divide or define the roles we play; our roles are more like the pieces of a puzzle. Ebbs and flows, ports and bays interconnect our existences. Now, multiply this to encompass the duration of an entire relationship, and it will look like a million-piece jigsaw. Not just one moment but a plethora of moments adjust to suit our greater needs and ultimately support to one another.

Viewing and embracing the beauty we bring over a duration of love and support reinforces the true nature of a healthy, loving, and supportive interaction with someone we love. It's also important to appreciate and acknowledge that this approach aligns with all types of relationships, including work, friend, team, and sports relationships, and every other possible variant that exists. Truth be known, to acknowledge and appreciate all our special gifts and interactions means embracing our roles in humanity.

Grasp with both hands the magnificence and beauty of the moment. For this exact moment will never be present again, and tomorrow brings with it a new, changed light. Rod xx

Photo - Jenni Mac

Imagine you, your life, and all its ingredients in a huge melting pot. The problem is you cook the good with all your previous difficult life moments, stewing in the difficulties, and saturating the pot with your problems. How do you change the way that you view your existence to lead to future healing? What if you exited that stew, no longer part of your past, and utilised all the ingredients from your life experiences to nurture yourself now and in the future?

Grab your ladle, and eat from your nutritional, abundant life. Feed yourself from your learnings, not living in your past but embracing the moments that gave you the knowledge and experiences to become who you are today: a beautiful, kind, giving, and loving individual. Respect, forgive, and be kind to yourself. Through this, healing begins, and happiness, love, and peace prevail.

The emotions of heartbreak, grief, and sadness

align with a significant moment of trauma in one's

experiences. During this period of heartbreak, nothing

else matters except the pain and personal suffering. We

generally feel as if our heart is literally breaking, but is

it truly breaking? Could that heartbreak, in fact, mean

the heart is healing? Think of it like the heart taking

a break from everything else while caring for itself

and recovering, or the heart actually breaking through

physical and spiritual barriers and connecting directly

to the Universe or heaven for the purpose of accessing

pure healing and universal love.

And as the rays of light like love disperse, a new shining

star can emerge and fill the heart once again with hope.

Through pain comes learnings, and once again, we

yearn to start the merry-go-round of love found and

love lost once again.

We all share a greater connection, and if we allow

ourselves to tap into this shared connection, we will get

abundant peace and happiness. The greatest element

that inhabits this realm is love, and if we just give

ourselves a moment and close our eyes, we can get

there. It's not difficult; we just need to believe.

I listened to a Divinyls song today ("Science Fiction"),
and I want to discuss the miracles it constantly
presented to me, provided you listen to it. In the song,
Chrissy Amphlett sings a line "Now that love is my
addiction". Hearing this, it occurred to me that, like any
other passion, if love is your addiction—not romantic
love but just pure love for all that is—then every fibre of
your being craves love.

When we feel love, what do we want to give? We want
to give ourselves—our complete selves. Imagine feeling
addicted to love, waking every day just wanting more
love. Remember, not specifically romantic love but love
between oneself and everything in between.

I have a vision of everyone giving love unconditionally
every day.

Question: How many days does it take to create a habit?
Let's make giving love a habit so we create passion.

What does love give in return? More love, peace,
happiness, health, and all things good.

Can we give this a go? Please add some more things that
love can do.

Give love, goodwill, generosity, gratitude, respect, and
kindness to all you come in contact with. Give your
loved ones a big hug, and tell them how much you love,
cherish, and adore them. Make love your addiction.

Thanks, Chrissy and everyone.

Our beauty and purity are like a sweet-smelling native

flower, floating in the wind and sharing its fragrance

with the Universe. It doesn't matter whom it touches;

just knowing that it sends out beauty and love, and

knowing that others can share it, is simply a beautiful

thing!

I wish everyone a beautiful, fragrant day.

Love,

Rod XXOO

Consciously or subconsciously, we all crave to be part

of something. We may believe we want to join another

individual or a collective, such as a profession. However,

if we take a step back and acknowledge our individual

strength, and know that we already have connections

to the greater Universe, we can be perfectly fine with

knowing ourselves and caring for ourselves. This is

not selfishness, as some might like you to believe, but

self-love. With self-love, self-belief, and self-respect, we

can care for our own island nation. Collectively, from

our own ruling nation, we can choose whom we allow

to enter our borders. This way of looking at things also

assists with an individual's boundary setting. Through

internal love and universal connectedness, we can share

love from the love and respect we have for ourselves

with purity, honesty, and safety.

I had an epiphany today (from the ancient Greek ἐπιφάνεια, epiphaneia, meaning "manifestation, striking appearance"—an experience of sudden and striking realisation). Generally, the term is used to describe scientific breakthroughs or religious or philosophical discoveries, but it can apply in any situation in which an enlightening realisation allows you to understand a problem or situation from a new and deeper perspective. When I write or speak, it appears I say things that have some meaning and purpose that give humanity hope and understanding of their connection with the Universe. But my head-mind didn't always see the significance of such philosophies. I battled within to determine why. *Was it truth? Where was the evidence?*

Then it dawned on me. Intuition, spirituality, connectedness, purpose, passion, love, and inner knowing, whether channelled through the spoken word or written down to share with the world, are just that: the Universe connecting, giving answers to share with the world for our true purpose. I failed to understand that the Universe doesn't communicate through mortal or physical senses. It doesn't speak or appear in a human form. It rests within us all. We don't hear it through our ears or see it with our eyes; we feel it, we sense it, and we are it. Find your quiet, and accept it, for within it lies all the answers. Don't overthink it or analyse it. Just be it. This is my epiphany, and I wanted to share it with you all.

I once had a vision and was encouraged to share it today.

As I looked out over the Universe, I could see planets and suns as far as my eyes could see. I looked around and noticed that a serpent-like creature was curled around the planets and suns as if protecting them. I looked down and noticed the closet planet was our Earth. On the surface of Earth, I saw little bonfires, and as I looked around, I saw a number of planets similar to our Earth. I asked myself, *What am I doing, and where am I?* A voice responded, letting me know I was viewing the Universe through the eyes of God, and the bonfires represented enlightened spirits on Earth. When all beings are enlightened on Earth, the Earth will become a sun and give life to new and developing planets in the Universe.

I'm sending you all some flint so that our creator may view you as a bonfire and continue Earth's and our progression in nurturing the rest of the Universe.

Love,

Rod XXOO

Do trees, or any other living things other than humans,

carry the weight of all their negative past experiences

in their current moment? They may have had exposure

to rough days, storms, and disasters, but they continue

to be what they are meant to be. If damage occurs, they

adapt and remain whole and don't stay in that past

moment. We, too, can gain nurturing from our past

experiences while not residing in our past. Accept the

spiritual nutrition from your colourful past, and use

the paint from your past to colour your now and your

future. Paint them the way you like them.

If we are really true to ourselves and mindful of what

we feel and why we feel it, and generally, if it is of a

negative nature, it connects to some period in the past.

What right does this past have to infiltrate our present

emotional stability, happiness, peace, and balance? If

we can alert ourselves that the past is not our present

life and has no purpose here, we also have the capacity

to put in back in its correct time zone. We don't need

to carry the past on our shoulders; the past is just

an ingredient that has assisted us in becoming the

complete people we are today. Just like when we make

a dish, we may include ingredients, but they shouldn't

stand out on their own. Some of these ingredients, if

exposed on their own, may not taste nice—such as pure

curry, for example. Would you stick a spoonful of curry

powder in your mouth? When included in a dish, curry

creates a beautiful experience that makes one's life

extraordinary.

When love and beauty is projected,
it is reflected upon the earth,
doubling the magic that transforms
the landscape from which it came.
When we project that which is not
of pure love, it is also doubled as it
is reflected. When the choice is of
love, purity is maintained. Love
multiplies love. Rod xx

Photo - Jenni Mac

In the midst of a plethora of monumental moments, one can experience either an overwhelming sense of the complex nature of our existence or an embracing and complete calm due to the beauty that exists and is presented to us daily, if not in every minuscule and immediate moment in time. We have the choice of which side of the precipice we wish to stand on. We can stand on the solid foundation of knowing all things are beautiful and universally gifted, or we can plummet into despair, where the foundation of peace, love, joy, and happiness will never be realised. What would you prefer? And how do we reach this?

Through our thoughts about and control of such things, we truly provide stability and calm. We choose to be happy, we choose to be love, and we choose and determine how we should feel.

Re-evaluate your present life. Modify and increase the components that generate happiness, and discard the stresses in your life. Your measure is not determined by sources that conspire to bring you down and keep you trapped in a life of mediocrity. You are beautiful, unique, gifted, and perfect. We all have the right to be perfect in everything we choose to do. All things should complement our lives, not diminish them. We should all strive for healthy interactions.

When one opens one's heart and protects it with a

pure intent, in every instance, equal love gravitates

toward and connects with the heart. Equality of love

and happiness exists for us all, and through emitting

love into the Universe, not unlike an antenna that only

picks up the higher vibrational frequencies of love, love

will be returned to us and shine on us once again. We

emit love generated from the spirit in many forms, and

one only has to grasp it and accept it for the healing to

manifest itself.

When one meanders through life and accepts one's path

as mundane, one will never experience the magic that

exists in never giving up. When doubt appears and a

cloud falls over your beliefs, continue striving, as magic

is everywhere, but you may miss it if you stop before

you turn the next corner.

My heart is mending and accepting and embracing

the truth. The greater lessons of attachment have

dissipated, and a warmth truth and blessings has

intertwined with my core belief. I'm being remoulded

and adapting again, as all manoeuvring spirits must do

as they transcend the Universe.

I forgive and love; therefore, I am forgiveness and love.

I will never allow my heart to fill up with another's turmoil; therefore, my heart remains at peace and only ever sends peace and purity of love to assist in others' healing. We have a direct connection to the Universe's healings, where your heart and all beautiful and loving hearts congregate to assist in the healing of all hearts and spirits. We only have to believe, and it will be just that—purity of all and ultimate healing, peace, tranquillity, and love. This is the place where love and magic are stored in abundance.

Dream and believe purity of love truly exists. It's yours for the taking. Honour it, love it, and embrace it.

XXOO

We all take our own personal journey filled with love, happiness, heartache, loss, pain, and everything in between. The parallel relations who endure the journey with us are the souls who have made contracts with us to return and share the learnings presented throughout these experiences. Some are simple lessons, and some catastrophic. The thing is, when such experiences present themselves to us, do we have the tools to deal with them in a way that assists us in embracing the turmoil associated with them? Such experiences occur regularly for humans. We can either delve into despair and lose the battle we chose to return for or utilise the gifts provided to us as our tools to conquer and succeed.

Our tools include using our parallel relationships, utilising the lessons provided, accepting our role, and making decisions to manoeuvre and combat with love, respect, forgiveness, and understanding. These tools act as our connecting conduit to our source and ultimate return ticket home. Some parallel relationships last for a lifetime and others for a very short period, but all have value and meaning, provided one is prepared to look deeply into the gift of having an opportunity to eventually get a relationship right. My parallel friendship will hopefully assist in guiding you on your magnificent and self-discovering journey.

It is sad that some people are prepared to throw away so much. It's perplexing to think that when beauty is the only thing that exists, some consider the option of immersing themselves in disturbing thoughts. When one fails to embrace the simplicity of pure intent, significant internal trauma results. We encounter many complex elements throughout our journey to realisation, and these are the true ingredients of our magical and colourful existence. When we embrace this and we take ownership of our own happiness, we accept our happiness is not connected to our past, and we do not hold on to blame or a victim status, allowing for true peace and enlightenment to manifest themselves.

Use your past as your paint to colour your canvas of today. Choose your colours, and paint the canvas as colourful or magical as you deem fit. Get it out, use it, and don't allow your past to fester within and create an internal storm and ultimate dysfunction. Use your paint, and colour your life, even if my name is Rod Painter. LOL. I couldn't help myself.

XXOO

Everything presents itself at its exact perfect moment.

Challenges and learnings are presented to us so we can

reach our truth of ultimate happiness. I'm sending you

love, strength, and resilience for your future successes.

Loving your children involves a constant balancing act, especially when they must work through some difficulties of their own. Slowly move in without their awareness, and hold them close, sending your heart and love to their hearts and spirits. Make them feel safe, give them some words of wisdom, and reassure them everything will be okay. Share with them how a wandering mind reduces one's capacity to stay present and how focusing energy on moments that either don't exist or don't yet exist reduces one's ability to use that energy to focus on the now, fight, and stay present. Return the energy to the moment so they maintain the capacity to endure.

My love for my children is my greatest gift and the greatest honour that has been bestowed on me. It is the purest love for all to embrace.

Your heart is a muscle, and not unlike how you build

any other muscle's strength, the heart needs to be

fatigued and stressed and broken down so stronger

repair can take place. A broken heart will once again get

strong. It's all about doing the work for greater healing

oneself.

Life serves us lessons that we're not supposed to easily

recognise or overcome, as only through us struggling

before reaching the other side can the lesson appear to

us. Amazing, though, how within struggles, beautiful

things can still appear. This is the magic of our

existence. Life is amazing, crazy, wonderful, and sad

and weaved with beauty if we open our hearts up to it.

Euphoria has emerged, engulfing the once-barren

landscape of a destitute heart. Alignment of the head

and heart contribute to this euphoria. To concretise

these significant elements of humans and spirits,

sit in a place of pure peace, and acknowledge their

magnitude; and in the same breath, acknowledge the

simplicity of these two truths.

When all facets of one's existence intertwine with all the

elements and purpose, beauty falls on us, providing us

with a hopeful, loving, and beautiful future. You could

say that in the darkest of moments, true clarity prevails,

and if prepared for and alert to the messages sent, then

only an uplifting and gifting experience can present

itself. Alignment of all and congruence of mind, heart,

and spirit will provide an abundance of purity, love,

peace, hope, and ultimately tranquillity.

When hope fades and deep pain brings you closer to

the source, you find the precipice alluring; however,

keep it out of reach. Reach out to the people who love

you, cherish you, and care for you. They bring you back

from the edge and cradle your heart. Don't give up;

fight. People need you and love you. You have a greater

purpose. Hold on until the sun shines again, because

it will, and you must endure. Do not own others'

contributions. You are pure and only exist of love. That

is your gift. Share it with the world.

It is amazing how people can just throw beauty away

when they are gifted it in their lives. They have no

concept of what others endure and struggle with due

to the significant pain and suffering they go through.

Appreciation and *gratitude* are just simple terms, but

they carry so much meaning in the hearts of those who

have lost beauty.

We have no greater gift or love than the love of family and friends. Through beautiful and genuine relationships, we develop respect and admiration when we come from a place of love. That love is the pinnacle of human existence. Love, in essence, is our existence beyond our human form, but when we accept it or give it from purity, our spirit resonates on Earth. Love connects the realms; love defines our existence. Love is where we come from and where we return to; love heals our physical and human trauma. We have love when no motive is otherwise present; that heals our physical heart.

When we share life's traumas with family and friends, and they share their love from a pure place, we can get no greater healing than through the medicine of love. Even though in times of significant trauma the physical cannot heal, love heals the spirit in preparation for what's next. Love is just that: LOVE ("long of varied existence", "levitating others' vibrational energy"). This is the path travelled throughout many a lifetime until love takes us home.

I'm sending love to all my family and friends who love me for my love, love me for my uniqueness, love me for my kindness, and love me for my heart. I thank you all for helping in my healing and acknowledging my special place in the world. I am blessed, and I am grateful for my life, my experiences, my family, my friends and my gorgeous children, who are my gift, my life, and my love.

We are sometimes gifted our experiences so we learn

a deep lesson about ultimately appreciating the

importance of self-love, kindness, boundary setting,

self-forgiveness, and forgiveness of others. This

provides for a happy heart and the key to accessing our

purpose and beauty.

Intuition, in all its grandeur, is an element of one's dimension that exists in all domains of reality. As we are aware, we can perceive reality through many complex components; one must seek balance when sharing both the physical and spiritual dimensions. When one solely relies on either physical tools or spiritual tools when navigating the complexities of our multi-layered existence, then one will experience flaws in the value of the experiences and challenges that present themselves, resulting in a view that may be tarnished by a narrowed viewpoint that fails to incorporate all dimensional input.

Embrace the love, and incorporate all the gifts offered to us that assist us in staying present now. It is the now that's important, and that's the true beauty of it.

Even in the darkest hour, if we look
deeply enough, there will always be a
light to guide our way. Rod xx

Photo - Jenni Mac

We can define the fortress of love in many ways. And if we think about boundary setting as an element of this, we can visualise our heart and our love within a castle and only permit the ones who are true to us, who enhance us, and who love us unconditionally to enter.

When we go searching for love externally to ourselves, we leave ourselves vulnerable to attack. When love attempts to search far away from itself in some distant land, and ultimately is not welcome, then we leave our fortress with no love connection, and it then has the potential to wither and lose its integrity.

Wisteria grows on the fortress's walls, as they have no maintenance, and a difficult path of reconnection manifests itself. Love those who love, connect with those who connect, venture far enough to maintain protection within the walls of your heart, and reel yourself back in to safety when another's love is not pure.

Mindfulness serves us well here also as the extension of thought. If we don't have the capacity to stay present, it takes us away from the moment and again leaves us vulnerable in a distant land of thought, where no good can be had at this exact time.

The energy of humanity exists on a spectrum whilst the

plectrum strums the fretboard bringing all into play.

There are master players that exist amongst us that can

play every tune and feel, communicate and broadcast

at every station available, and some that can only tune

into one station at a time sending out their song.

We as humans have the gift to communicate with

human language, with our human senses, but not

necessarily to all with energy alone, hence the

alignment to the equally aligning entities where

friendships and bonds are forged.

We can expand our repertoire of energy levels through

the internal song of love, gentleness, respect and

kindness, and the expansion of our energy brings us

closer to the purity of spirit, and assists in the tuning

of detuned entities struggling to find their way through

the maze of this experience we call life.

Hey just wanted to let you know I arrived safely, the weathers great and the waters warm, and the people and the food are just beautiful. I have seen some amazing sites and a sunken wreck, but there is one thing missing, and of course, that is you.

I watch the sun go down, glistening over the ocean as it says good night to the day and its sister moon gently waves goodnight bringing a beautiful sea breeze through my window, whilst the memory of your perfume wafts through the corridors of my mind, bringing a heart filled tear to the surface, as I feel it running down my cheek.

Not a heartbeat goes unnoticed as I watch the clock tick awaiting a brand new day, and I venture out awaiting the world to wake, witnessing the dawn and the magic as the bats and owls say goodnight and a sea turtle ventures back into its ocean home.

I lay on the sand and hear the waves licking the sand and the warmth of Mother Earth comes from both within and from the sun as I feel it peeking over the horizon. There's magic here in the storybook of my mind, and the memory vaults of my heart. However, if it is only me that has the pleasure of viewing and feeling it daily without sharing, can become routine and isolating. So would like to invite you to share the holiday of my dreams, and embrace this brand new day with love and magic.

Just be as you be and the most perfectly aligning bee

will connect and return together to the mother hive. As

we venture and grow, searching for that perfect nectar,

we will undoubtedly connect with perfection and love

and embrace the beautiful fragrances gifted.

Throughout our humanity, we are made up of many

hives, differing species, with varied drives and focus. So

important to be mindful when connecting with aligning

perfection so that only beauty is manifested whilst here

in physical form.

And until we return to the collective hive where we're

ultimately in perfect alignment, live in beauty, in

kindness, respect and understanding and we'll all have

access to happiness, love and peace.

The magic of connection ideally is what we crave, desire and constantly search for. However it is so important that the connection once established is pure, deep and mutual. Humanity and its reinforced notion of shallow relationships will constantly trip us up, as we will always exist in a place of mistrust, and attempt to hold on and ultimately reside in a place of loss.

It is only when letting go, that heartache disperses and the emotion of loss no longer has a hold of our hearts. Pure connections are greater than our human experiences, and will continue beyond our physical, so loss is never part of that equation when we have that sense that our connections will continue beyond this realm and into the next.

Without a doubt, our human makeup will allow us to feel the trauma as it is presented, but to acknowledge the greatness beyond, will assist in generating our peace, our continued love and the embracing of the constant beauty presented.

One's narrative is generally formed from all life experiences, but also from a life of being on autopilot and allowing the tarnish of ones history to continue to rust one's life today, and into the future. We have all been exposed to a plethora of experiences and it is generally the negative ones that stick like rust if we allow it to, and these are the elements that hinder our potential relationships into the future.

But one community member, one person from a particular faith, one person from a particular culture, one person that has done us wrong, doesn't speak or act for the collective and for the greatness that potentially could be had.

It's amazing how we restrict beautiful opportunities for connection based on our history, and absolutely self-preservation, self-care, self-love is paramount in the protection of one's heart. But if we embrace the learnings and not fall back into those same patterns, take it slow, really get to know before investing the vulnerabilities of your heart, then we shift our narrative to one of strength and wisdom.

We can rebuild and rust proof ourselves. We just need to be mindful and present, and only switch on autopilot when safety of love has been proven, validated and enduring.

Could it be that love is the overarching power of all of our universes elements, and when true it will wear down the greatest rock formation, greatest wall, all ills, and make a path directly to one's heart, and nothing can hold back its power.

Could it also be that due to humanities manipulation of love and subsequent greed, power and self-obsession, that its power in the form of all elements are constantly attempting to cleanse the misalignment, and in the process innocents are also impacted upon, and not only humanity, but all living creatures.

And until we all align in the truth, purity, magic and wonder of love then the universe will continue to rectify and cleanse, generating an environment of fear and uncertainty. It is through the purity of love and its subsequent beauty when spread throughout the world that the beauty of the world and all its inhabitants will endure.

This kind of aligning love is the only love I hope to accept, and the only love I believe all humans deserve. Never settle and listen deeply to your intuition, we all possess this gift and it will serve us well, providing we listen deeply to its message in the silence of our hearts.

It's important to be mindful when sending out love into

the world that the universe doesn't misconstrue it as

a mayday call, as what you send out is returned. Like

a submarine sending sonar, it needs to come from the

engine room and not the shell.

If sent from the shell it fails to heal oneself first,

ultimately resulting in depletion. If sent purely from

ones heart then it resonates from the core dispersing

through ones internal space before healing the world.

Be perfectly beautiful as you are and mindful that it's

not an SOS in the seeking of love, as desperation will be

what is pinged and returned. Nothing but love.

As we're exposed we'll adapt, and every moment in between is meant to be exactly as it should be. We sometimes sit in a place thinking if only? If only this was different, what if I was to change that, why can't I be like that person and the list goes on.

And if one desires then so shall it be. But until then it's exactly as it is. We meet people, we love people, we lose people, all the whilst we are growing, expanding, and getting a greater sense and getting in touch with ourselves.

The defining element here is us and now, we can't be anymore then what we are at is exact moment, so embrace this amazing and magical beauty that is us right at this moment, and things will be as they be in perfect harmony. You are beautiful in every way now, but like a chameleon, we morph as the passages of time present, exactly as it's meant to be.

In a perfect world, healthy attachments should be ones birth right, a natural progression from birth that supports the transition into adulthood, that again is perpetuated in healthy romantic relationships and ideally the cycle continues and the world is a beautiful, loving and peaceful place. But the equilibrium of the world is out of kilter, and all its Inhabitants are continually attempting to adapt to a world where balance on the greater scale is no longer a given.

So humanity is born into struggle, and trust and love are things to be suspicious of. And if and when it ever arrives, ones history would say the motives of the other are flawed, and will run, and generally into the arms of someone who is also tarnished, that then reinforces that trust and love have a price, pain and suffering endures, and the push and pull of love remains. A number of options exist. Continue down the path of pursuance of love, and get burnt, learn and ideally find perfection? Close shop, or if any attempts made, never commit for the fear of being let down and living in a state of angst. Settle for less than deserving, in the hope it'll be ok, and not too diminishing or soul destroying and the list goes on.

Ideally all we want is to be loved by a significant other, feel safe, have security and know that we won't be betrayed, and pure intentioned trust to run both ways. I don't believe any of us are naive enough to think that these types of connections will exist forever, but for many the purity and duration of love remains a lifetime and that's a beautiful thing, and one we all strive for, but to communicate feelings throughout any process is of paramount importance, decency and respect.

And this is the karma ideally we're putting back into

the world. Feelings of isolation and disregard, when we

are a species of energetic love connections, are I feel

some of the most debilitating and heart destroying

experiences to endure. So be mindful in love and

friendship, and of the sensitivities of others, as their

experiences vary and pain very close to the surface,

or deep awaiting to be healed. Sending out love and

forgiveness, in the hope that love and forgiveness will

be returned to all.

We will never truly know the thoughts and feelings of another, especially when both the other and oneself are not always true to themselves. Even when we think and believe we are being honourable, the recipient is drawing from their own experience and formulating their own feelings around that exact interaction. Without the opportunity of brut honesty in the form of communication, and dialogue within an environment of safety and trust, one will generate not only one possible outcome, but a multiple of variables that ideally and hopefully lead back to a place of deep reflection when that opportunity of brut honesty is unavailable.

Ones blocking is a safety mechanism with a belief that all their experiences have culminated to this exact moment and the tarnish of time reinforces that exact notion. The three truths ring true in an environment such as this. Their truth, your truth and the real truth. In counselling this clarity ideally allows an individual to empathise another's potential thought outcomes, and alleviate the stressors placed on one's own heart, especially if honour and truth was ideally the motivation. Truth in Communication is the only alleviator of miscommunication.

We possess wisdom, intellect, kindness, compassion, love, and understanding. But none of these attributes can immediately nullify an aching heart. The experiences of grief and loss come in many shapes and forms. And some answers around the experience are present and some never to be known.

Still the pain is the same but the healing time varied based on each individuals experiences. Closure within the psyche can appear more expediently when the reasons known, however a spiralling may manifest when clarity is not available.

As humans we like a sense of control, and when control is taken away confusion prevails. The thing is we will not always know so acceptance of the unknown and the accompanying feelings are our greatest ally. Feel completely and think of love and pure intent, and healing will be its ultimate outcome and gift.

Immerse in your heart as it's here where all beautiful memories reside. All loved ones lost, current love and all love still to be had. It's your heart that is the conduit across all time and space, and if we bath in this beautiful space and put our human ails aside, we can feel, truly feel the depth and meaning of love.

In the joy of love and the angst of love is when we really feel the truth of the universe and our part in its greatness, and tap into the many facets of feeling. This is when we are truly alive, no routines, no schedules, just being, present, connected and loved. Go to this place in meditation and on resurfacing the remnants of divinity (LOVE) will be your constant companion. My heart beats of love, as do us all, and deserves to heal the world and all its inhabitants. Share it graciously.

Fear is that mountain that many feel they are unable or unwilling to climb. But fear is an illusion and when challenged the mountain becomes smaller and smaller, and the angst of the potential struggle diminishes. We view people that have success in many spheres, professionals, the arts and even ones in love as having gifts that are special, unique and greater then we can ever possess.

And yes certain gifts are aligned with a certain

few, but the true gift is fearlessness. There's truly a

simplistic notion of just being and aligning with the

things one loves in all or any capacity, providing love,

kindness, respect and gratitude are its foundation. From

grandiose if one desires to a Zen like calm and relaxed

existence.

We all have our roles, and that is to be exactly who we

be, no more no less, and align with the souls that allow

us to be exactly that with no expectation or pressure

to be anything different but ourselves. It is when we

resonate with our truth that the waves of beauty spread,

and that love and alignment assists in the healing and

minimisation of fear so only ones greatness prevails. No

fear in love, only Love.

Have you ever wondered when you're feeling blue and melancholy filled, of what the emotion could be trying to tell you. Generally, it leads us to a place of sadness and loss, of times passed, a current dilemma, or future focused stresses. But mainly we make it about us, why me? How come? and commence the spiralling into negativity, and no doubt many of ones truths weaved throughout.

But I had a moment today when it felt like the earth, humanity and all of our universes inhabitants that are under stress were calling out for support and love. Could it be that for the ones with a greater sensitivity, feel the calling of the universe to bandy together, and instead of internalising the suffering, externalise the love, and send it back into the universe for healing.

I have no doubt that the energetic waves of love when sent from the masses of empathic souls will wash over the tragic events and assist in the healing, that we all have a responsibility to do. It's from the giving of love to the collective when the collective returns the healing and love, and transforms all our experiences into one of divinity as it was meant to be. Karma in real time. Just try it!

*Even in the distance the
beauty is still innately in
the present. Why wait to
embrace a beautiful
distant emotion, when it
can be had in this
moment? There is only
the now, so feel the love.
Rod xx*

Photo - Jenni Mac

In the shell of our humanity, we feel captured and closed, and also fearful that if our shell was abandoned we would ooze out and no longer be anything of substance. So we close ourselves in staying within the confines of what we believe to be our protection, but in actual fact these are our illusional prison walls.

In unhealthy relationships, in work we don't enjoy, we continue to walk the worn path, wanting change but still having the fear of that unknown element so dare not tread that path of mystery and potential magic. The step of change doesn't have to be physical in nature, but thought driven, spiritual in essence. Freedom is not necessarily standing on a mountain top with no human desires and living a zen like existence, even though that sounds divine.

But it's a way of being, a way of focus, a way of thought and a way to destiny. Whilst in human form we still need to do the human dance, but can still be free in our hearts and spirit, and can tap into the magic whilst we pursue our personal passions and loves. Admittedly if relationships are toxic in any environment one may need to relocate, reposition, re-evaluate and a forced move prevails, which could also be part of our greater lessons and gifted wisdoms from the universe when pushed in such a way. Freedom of heart and spirit is ours to embrace and we can soar no matter where we are, we just need to believe in the magic that is present and love! As love is the key to all magic.

More and more the constructs of self-love are reinforced, and always heightened when ones defences are lowered for the sharing of human love and forgiveness. Humans will inevitably disappoint, make mistakes, and talk behind your back, in the attempt to bring you down, whilst believing they are raising their status and truth in the world.

The thing here is to be congruent of your own truth, purity of action and self-belief, and not allow another's behaviour to minimise or determine your value. It surely rocks you, and your first instinct is to react and justify, maybe even fall into the same game. But this approach won't serve you well, so go to your safe place, meditation, music, exercise, therapy, the beach, painting, art, singing, a bush walk, nature, write, a phone call to family or a friend, the movies, cafe, your favourite series, or wherever it is you feel inspired and at peace, and equilibrium will again return.

Pure Universal love flows through us, we came from here and will eventually return, but our human experiences of love are the tests we born ourselves into, and no doubt when we return we'll calculate how long it took us to find our peace and our pure love whilst in human form. Always testing, always growing, always in the pursuit of love.

Why is it that it appears everyone else knows ours strengths, attributes, skills, worth, more then we believe ourselves. How often do your friends, families, colleagues share how wonderful you are, beautiful you are, kind you are, gentle you are? Can we see a trend happening here? There is a mould, an aligning component that comes with all these traits, and that's a innate sensitivity, not only in understanding the outside world, but a deeper connection to ones own inner sensitivities and ultimate vulnerabilities.

The truth here is we don't want the world to truly know our vulnerabilities so we suffer alone. We're meant to be the strong ones, the ones that everyone comes too for their strength. We know we are special, but fail to connect deeply, again because of the fear of hurt and disappointment. So instead of allowing things to grow, we slowly decay inside, all the whilst hiding it away from the ones we love, due to the pedestal they place us on.

Certainly scary and a balancing act, and people that possess these beautiful sensitivities don't always have the best help seeking behaviours, as that may be misconstrued as a sign of weakness, but quite the contrary, should be embraced as strength and inner growth.

Don't ever change, but important to be mindful of these characteristics and continually strive to find that balance that enhances that greatness, and seek support when required to rebalance. The body responds and heals to massage, and touch, the same as the mind and spirit responds to love and connection. A hearts stresses shared is a heart stresses halved.

Another day opens like a page from a book, and the moonbeams hide away awaiting the sparkle of the sun to have its glory shining over the world. And in some tranquil location the rain drops spread to assist a developing rainbow send its magic to touch the hearts of us all that only want love, all the whilst all the souls beat in harmony awaiting their moment to do what their destined to do, to be of perfection, be of magic, doing the symbiotic dance of the universe.

We are all part of that perfection, and need to embrace and align with the dance and complement its healing and the expansion of the love to all living creatures. And as one breathes another exhales, and as one moves, another flows with the breeze that's generated.

And as the moon rises again and the tides shift, and the creatures of the day bed down for the night, they make way for their nocturnal brothers and sister to emerge, and another cycle of life and universal alignment begins. Flow with the love and tide of the magic we're born into, don't fight it, don't destroy it, admire it, bath in it, embrace it, and it'll embrace and love you in return. Only love.

You know the mind boggles when you learn how to deeply reflect on the learnings and lessons constantly gifted. Whilst in the centre of trauma clarity generally fails us, but if we trust in the universes perfection, and allow the experience to pass through us and not hold on to the residuals of that moment passed, can be an absolute cleansing that presented for that exact purpose.

And if we delve to the core we can appreciate that whatever presented has highlighted our attachments, our impatience, our human foibles and the greater learnings for the development of our ultimate peace and internal happiness. Unhealthy attachments of our past experience can and will build up generating a toxic filled waste, that will only protrude collecting additional waste and saving for future trauma ignition.

To forgive is to cleanse, to cleanse is to be free, to be free is to be weightless, happy and peaceful. Visualising the waves of forgiveness and love moving through washing away the toxicities, and embracing the greatness and magic that exists within us all.

Love is pure, love is peaceful, love is kind, love is happiness, love is connectedness, love is all-knowing, love is an ocean. However throughout our human passage it appears we sail on that ocean of love, where the land we came from is love, and the destination after our voyage is completed lands us on a continent of love once again.

But whilst here we attempt to captain that vessel of our humanity falling to fall deeply into the depths of that ocean of love we sail upon. It's of utmost importance to captain our humanity and navigate the many reefs and shallows, however it's of equal importance to immerse in the love that many of us just sail upon.

Absolutely there's magic in our humanity, and many atrocities also, however it's in the depths and the silence of love where those two lands meet is the all-knowing, our peace, our happiness, our purpose and our love, which is ideally what we're all striving for. Why wait until that land is found, when if we walk that plank and jump it's all ours for the taking. Enjoy the dip of tranquillity.

A new dawn breaks and my eyes open again, another

day down and getting stronger every day. Reflections of

days now passed when love was supposed to conquer

all, and dreams shared to never be realised. The aches

of our past are deep within our bones, but must be

purged for our hearts healing.

Open your heart and expose your fears, I know you're

scared but I'm right beside you, you're truly never

alone if you become best friends with your fears and

vulnerabilities. So share your heart because that's

where it's starts without a beginning there is no end,

let it soar fly and be free, and once it's healed bring it

back to me. Only my deepest love being sent, mirrored,

expanded and returned.

There's a warmth a gentleness a simplicity that

manifests when one is of truth and of love. If we can

learn to strip back the build-up and residuals of our

past lives, without an expectation of what's in it for me

mentality, a pureness of existence prevails.

To be in touch with our core, our spirit will inevitably

bring us closer to the beautiful connections we can all

share, without the tarnished ravages that our humanity

can sometimes bestow upon us. Visualise immersing

into a deep well of love and allow a detoxification

and cleansing of life's struggles wash away, and then

surfacing back into the world rejuvenated, and like

perfection as you were once born.

True beauty and purity of love exist only within the

hearts of the pure. Healing manifests and love prevails

only when one's actions align with all things pure, right,

and just.

Wow!

Our mission is the pursuance of love, happiness and connection. It is through our connection of energy when all these elements align. Through purity of intent, one of goodness, kindness, forgiveness & love, our capacity to endure and develop an appreciation of all things beautiful is manifested and maximized for us all to embrace. A dilemma is presented however when ones' heart is injured, a human experience, as the energy invested is depleted as soon as its nourished, without the capacity to stay whole and complete. Not unlike a balloon that has a slow leak. We can keep blowing and blowing, but as soon as we stop the balloon will go flat and lifeless. Our hearts work in a very similar way if we fail to correct the wound at its core level. We sometimes over-think and create complex situations, when in fact if we go back to the simplistic notion of our spirit and align with the purity of our spirit, our human manifestation will connect with all that is perfect and align with what's rightfully ours to embrace and love.

Sending love and healing energy to your heart. Rod xxoo

We have to deal with grief and loss, relationship breakups, mental illness & injuries that all impact on our hope and happiness, and during the experiences we can spiral out of control and lose perspective on how simple it is to get it all back in balance. It's like swimming against the rapids, getting exhausted and drowning in despair. The only result will be a furthering of the inner torment and ultimate sadness, unhappiness and illness. The alternative may be to float with the current. It's going to be a bumpy ride, but if we ride it without a fight until we get to the calm waters, we can crawl up on the shore, shake ourselves off and move forward, factoring in the experience and learning the lessons that the universe is providing us. Thank you so much for taking the time to read,, and allowing me to share some of my life and the things gifted to me to share with you.

Love, heart & hugs. Rod xxoo Some people have magnificent explosions of awareness and others come and go and tinker with the idea that this experience is the bridge into the next. The question is, do we wish to just walk aimlessly across that bridge and falling off before reaching true enlightenment or do we experience every moment and reach the other side with our purpose and spirit intact? The reason you're reading this now is because it's your time and every experience you have is about the growth and learning and through this what can you give back.

Somewhere along this bridge, when everything is receptive and open to change, the learning will present itself. It may be subtle, but it's when we're prepared that these visions or opportunities will be picked up, a bit like intuition or six sense. Be open to these opportunities and allow them to flow through you. Before you fall into the peace and tranquillity of meditation request the answers of your purpose and just give in to the response. If you don't know then just give in, as the answer are awaiting your question. All the answers are available and we have access to them all. The knowledge of the Universe is flowing within us. It's not separate to us as if we have to travel there. We can tap into this abundance of knowledge and happiness, peace and prosperity. We just have to ask. When things get tough, ask for the answer. Lay back and float for a while, not allowing yourself to get chewed up by the overlapping confusion. Give in to the collective and the answers will be there.

With Love. Rod xxoo